Seeking Solace

# Seeking Solace

### Finding Hidden Miracles and Peace
### When Life Doesn't Go as Planned

## Chani Barlow

NEW YORK

LONDON • NASHVILLE • MELBOURNE • VANCOUVER

# Seeking Solace

## Finding Hidden Miracles and Peace When Life Doesn't Go as Planned

Published in New York, New York, by Morgan James Publishing. Morgan James is a trademark of Morgan James, LLC. www.MorganJamesPublishing.com

Scripture quotations are taken from the King James Version of the Bible, public domain.

This material is neither made, provided, approved, nor endorsed by Intellectual Reserve, Inc. or The Church of Jesus Christ of Latter-day Saints. Any content or opinions expressed, implied or included in or with the material are solely those of the owner and not those of Intellectual Reserve, Inc. or The Church of Jesus Christ of Latter-day Saints.

Proudly distributed by Ingram Publisher Services.

**Morgan James BOGO™**

A **FREE** ebook edition is available for you
or a friend with the purchase of this print book.

_____

CLEARLY SIGN YOUR NAME ABOVE

**Instructions to claim your free ebook edition:**
1. Visit MorganJamesBOGO.com
2. Sign your name CLEARLY in the space above
3. Complete the form and submit a photo
   of this entire page
4. You or your friend can download the ebook
   to your preferred device

ISBN 9781631957963 paperback
ISBN 9781631957970 ebook
Library of Congress Control Number:
2021948060

**Cover Design by:**
Rachel Lopez
www.r2cdesign.com

**Interior Design by:**
Chris Treccani
www.3dogcreative.net

Morgan James PUBLISHING

**Builds**

with...

**Habitat for Humanity**
Peninsula and
Greater Williamsburg

Morgan James is a proud partner of Habitat for Humanity Peninsula
and Greater Williamsburg. Partners in building since 2006.

Get involved today! Visit MorganJamesPublishing.com/giving-back

# Contents

Acknowledgments ........................................... *vii*

Introduction ............................................... *ix*

Empty Room ................................................ 1

The Good Kid .............................................. 3

The Lucky One ............................................. 15

I Hate Waiting ............................................. 25

This Was Different ......................................... 37

An Inspired Message ....................................... 43

Adoption Day .............................................. 49

A Day in the Life .......................................... 65

Fulfillment ................................................ 73

The Dream ................................................. 75

Hannah .................................................... 83

Time to Move On ........................................... 95

The Coca-Cola Store ....................................... 111

Her Name .................................................. 119

Gender Reveal ............................................. 123

At the Hospital ............................................ 129

Oh, the Joy ................................................ 141

A Birthday Present ......................................... 149

Someone Is Missing ........................................ 159

Think of a Name on the Way ................................ 173

Find Her .................................................. 187

Decisions and Setbacks ..................................... 195

Youth Harbor .............................................. 205

The Little Ones ............................................ 215

Some Doubts                                          221
What's Best                                          227
Now What Do I Do?                                    241
Baby Girl                                            247
Conclusion                                           263
Thank You                                            267

*About the Author*                                   *269*
*End Notes*                                           *271*

# Acknowledgments

To my Calliope Writing Tribe: Amy, Angie, thank you for cornering a somewhat hesitant mom and infusing her with confidence, encouragement, and permission to fail. You were my first step in the right direction. More than coincidence. I know now that I needed to find you.

To Eschler Editing: How does a first timer even go about finding a professional editor? Three trusted mentors, all separate from each other, personally recommended your team. I heartily add my voice as a fourth and then some. Liz, Michele, Angela, thank you for embracing my story and the message I wanted to share. You polished my words and smoothed the rough patches. Your final touches elevated the entire manuscript.

To my friends at Morgan James: Not everyone can say that they start their career on a "dream team," but I certainly can. Terry, thank you for taking a chance on a squeaky, nervous pitch. Heidi and Shannon, you've been so patient to hold my hand through the process. Jim, your ideas and expertise made it real. I never told you, but I almost cried after our first call. David, I'm proud to know you and learn directly from you. To the designers, guerrillas, authors, mentors, and all the rest of the dream team: I'm so impressed by what you do daily. Thank you for helping create miracles.

To my countless friends, babysitters, beta readers: I couldn't have done any of this without you! There are too many of you to name! Thank you for giving me your precious time and feedback so willingly. I'm incredibly blessed to have you in my life.

To my mental health team: I've never felt better. Sam, thank you for letting me spew out the yuckiest parts of myself and not flinching. I am a better person because of our discussions.

To my boys: I'm so proud of you. Thank you for letting mom shut the bedroom door and type until late. I've been able to relive those phone calls and when we first brought you home. It gets me every time. Love you guys!

To Keith: You always told me I should write. Thank you for believing in my talents long before I dusted them off and put them to use. Thank you for taking over bedtime, even on the wildest nights. You nudge me forward, offering to take each step right alongside me. Together, we are a formidable force! I love you, Buggy.

To my Heavenly Father: Thank you for whispering that it was time to share our story, and for all the coincidences and mercies that led us here. You've opened doors when I hit dead ends and you let me sob irrationally when I didn't always understand. Through it all, I know you're there. This book has always been your story, not mine.

# Introduction

This is a story about miracles—enormous miracles so unexplainable and impossible I'm still shaking my head and dozens of tiny little miracles, dreams, and coincidences. God's hand is in all of it. But this is not just my story. This is your story too.

I wrote this book for you.

I tried to picture you hiking alongside me wearing your comfiest clothes and squinting in the sun. We might wave to other early risers passing us on the trail, but other than that, we would talk openly. I'd offer you a water bottle, expose some of my parenting missteps, and trust that you wouldn't turn the other way. You might nod, understanding and sympathy creasing your face. You would share some of the nuggets of wisdom your parents passed along to you. We'd ask each other meaningful questions about our lives. That's what friends do. We'd have a conversation.

This book is my side of our conversation.

My story is unique to me, just as yours is unique to you. I've only lived my one life in my little corner of the world. Though our journeys vary in the details, there is much that is the same. In sharing my story, I hope you begin to see the little miracles in your journey—even if you don't believe in miracles.

My greatest wish is that in sharing and acknowledging our best and worst moments, we'll find connection within ourselves, with God, and with each other. I'll be your safe place if you'll be mine.

Warmly,
Chani
November 2021

# Empty Room

## Summer 2006

I unraveled the blankets from my legs and wandered down the hallway, looking for the little girl from my dreams. I don't know what I expected to find. Maybe the ethereal outline of a toddler standing in the hallway, a white nightgown dusting the tops of her tiny bare feet. Maybe I hoped for a waft of pink Johnson & Johnson's baby lotion. She wasn't there. Of course she wasn't. But her presence was so palpable I couldn't help but check to make sure.

She had visited my dreams again, coaxing me awake before 3:00 a.m. Those blue eyes, those strikingly light-blue eyes rimmed with a shock of lush black lashes, seared into my consciousness. They gazed up at me from flawless, ivory skin. They recognized me. Her dark, curly hair framed her face, wild and free, mirroring her whimsical expressions. I knew that face well, and, yet, I had no idea who she was.

I could have escorted myself back to my bed; my exhausted body would have welcomed a soft pillow and a chance to drift away with my arms around my sweetheart. Instead, I glanced at the door to the third bedroom, which was completely empty except for the desk I'd built with my dad when I was twelve. The door remained shut most of the time. I'd like to say I opened it to dust and vacuum regularly, but I didn't. I avoided it.

*You're ridiculous, Chani. You know that?* I scolded myself as I sat on the landing of the stairs, stretching out my legs. The quiet of the house yielded to the buzz of the refrigerator and the whisper of the breeze against the windowpanes. All noise and yet completely silent.

I arched my back, feeling my lower spine pinch. I rubbed at it, trying to ignite the courage to stand up, retrace my steps to my bedroom, and lie down next to my husband. He didn't know that when I closed my eyes each night, the dark-haired girl waited for me, begging me to find her. It wasn't that I was afraid to tell him about her. I just didn't know how.

Where would we even begin to look for her?

I leaned against the wall, balancing the weight of my head on the messy ponytail jutting out from behind my neck.

Really, she could be anywhere, in any country. She might not even be born yet.

I closed my eyes, listening to the air conditioner softly humming through the vents above me. I gripped the hem of my ratty T-shirt in my fist. I wanted to hold her close enough to feel her dark curls tickling my chin. I needed to press her full cheeks up against mine and promise her that there would be no more empty bedrooms with closed doors. She was my daughter.

*It doesn't matter where she is. I will do anything, go anywhere, to find her. Look how far I've already come . . .*

# The Good Kid

*December 2, 1995*

I sat cross-legged in newly washed jeans in front of my bedroom mirror. For the last hour, I'd coaxed my stubbornly-straight blonde hair into the curling iron. I smeared on a wide streak of black eyeliner and spritzed my neck with Vanilla Fields perfume.

I'd been to plenty of church dances and the sixth-grade "I'll sign your dance card if you sign mine" end-of-year celebration, but my card never filled up. I spent a lot of time in a bathroom stall so Mr. Barber wouldn't catch on that nobody wanted to dance with the spelling-bee runner-up. But this was a new day, my first real high school dance.

Most people only knew me for my worn gym shoes and sweaty T-shirts. My petite frame deceived every sprinter who set down their starting block in the lanes next to me. The last one to take position at the starting line, I shook my stubby legs. They always underestimated me. I loved it. I didn't even register on their radars. When my mispronounced name blasted over the loudspeaker, they looked around, narrowing their eyes only to discover that the underdog had blown past them. *Nice one, Mr. Announcer. It's Chani (SHAW-knee). You'll be saying you knew me back in the day.*

I swayed in front of the mirror as Richard Marx serenaded me from my boom box. If I ever broke through my invisibility and noncheerleader status, Taylorsville High School would gasp, dazzled by the shinier, more interesting version of me. A new sweater.

The perfect jeans. Lip gloss! My elephant necklace pressed comfortingly against my chest, reminding my heart to take it easy.

I checked the alarm clock on the windowsill. My throat pinched at the thought of arriving late. I swallowed and steadied my breathing. I took the stairs two at a time, only to perch on the arm of the couch, my forehead stamping a Revlon smudge on the window, as I waited for my ride. I'd once heard George Washington allowed only five minutes "for differences in watches" because tardiness showed disrespect. That was me. My friends Jennie and Tara humored my compulsive earliness. Jennie's mom, Mrs. Simpson, honked as she pulled into the driveway. She smiled a big, toothy grin, snapped on her gum, and fluttered her bright-red fingernails at me through the window as I ran up and pulled on the door handle.

At the school, we ducked underneath the blue-and-gold "Go Warriors" banner to catch the dance committee still stringing streamers from the basketball hoops to the wall. The DJ repositioned his speakers and taped down the trailing cords in the silent gym. The chaperones in the corner donned Christmas sweaters well before it was trendy to own them. Nobody even looked up. We left, desperate not to seem so desperate.

Twilight settled in over the pitiful mounds of dirty, melted snow still stubbornly clinging to the sidewalks and streets. My short brown boots fishtailed with each step, the heels trying to find solid, dry ground. We looped around the edge of the football field, the sound of traffic roaring louder with each step we took toward the main road. I folded my fingers into the cavernous sleeves of my striped sweater and shivered. I could see the red-and-green lights strung from the Mexican restaurant across the street. The Walmart sign buzzed just behind it. For a microsecond, I thought, *No, don't go. Don't do it.* But I ignored it, justifying the intense need for a pack of peppermint gum from the store. Certainly, we could be back before the DJ played "With or Without You."

I glanced indifferently at the cars whizzing past us on the left and right. I stood back just enough to avoid the tires spraying blackened slush onto the sidewalk and patted my back pocket, checking for my school ID. We could have turned left, taking the unlit path in front of the angled, modern apartments. Far too scary in the shadows. We could have turned right, walking more than a block to the crosswalk at the intersection, but the lights took forever, and cars didn't pause anyway, not even for pedestrians. We hesitated, chewing on our freshly painted jade fingernails and glancing back at the parking lot, now starting to welcome a few more cars.

Without a traffic light, our bus usually sat at this same corner for a solid ten minutes before ramming straight across, spilling us into the aisle with Pop-Tart crumbs and pebbles dislodged from the treads of our shoes. We could cross in no time at all.

I popped my knuckles inside my sleeves and tapped the toe of my boot against the curb. I noticed spots of black ice on the road and made a mental note to avoid them. Catching a brief lull in the traffic, we grabbed each other's hands, giggling as we dashed across the first few lanes, a real-life version of the classic arcade game Frogger. No crosswalk. No yellow flashing lights. Halfway there. We paused in the left turn lane to wait for the cars to clear in the opposite direction. An endless train of holiday headlights streamed past us.

Without warning, Tara darted out, leaving Jennie and me in her wake. I reached for her billowing shirt, leaning forward as far as possible to try to pull her back. I missed. I screamed her name, but it lodged in my throat. I pivoted in time to see headlights surging toward me. Bright lights. The tires didn't even screech. I shielded my face and braced for the impact.

I felt like I was underwater, the sounds, lights, smells all muted. I knew I was lying in the road. My nose brushed against the loose pebbles, and my forehead was pinned to a painted white stripe. Why? No idea. I heard myself taking deep, even breaths as I pried my eyes open. The shouting and the flashing lights blurred as I focused on a single puddle of blood a few inches from my cheek. An occasional crimson drop rolled off my eyebrow and into the puddle. *Drip, drip, drip.*

I reached up and tenderly touched my forehead, then held my palm close to my face. Sticky, wet blood stained my shaky fingers. I raised my head, willing my vision to clear. Lights. Lots of lights. And cold. Very, very cold. I begrudgingly raised myself into a half-hearted push-up, the kind I did when the morning alarm went off. Forceful hands shoved my backside down. "Stay still!" a voice commanded.

Someone vaguely familiar tucked a red Mario Bros sleeping bag around me and sat on the pavement next to me. Why did they ask me about basketball? How did they know about my preseason game against Midvale on Friday? I mumbled something about running ladders at practice, but then my words coagulated as they rolled off my lips. Suddenly exhausted, I surrendered to sleep. I couldn't help it. To this day, I have yet to learn who wrapped me up and grounded me with talk of basketball while the firefighters and EMTs swirled around me, trying to assess the damage.

I jolted awake and found myself lashed to a gurney. A red-headed EMT loaded me into an ambulance, banging my gurney against the bumper of the ambulance so the wheels collapsed. Then he climbed in and steadied the bed with one leg while reaching for items in the boxes on the shelves. How did one install shelves inside a car? I eyed the man closely. How did the senior class president have time to be an EMT? Did he get school credit for riding along in the ambulance? Was I making him miss the Stomp? If I ran my fingers through my semicurled hair, would it distract him from the fact that I had one short sock and one long? What underwear was I wearing? Was he actually there?

In the emergency room, a game show played on the TV. The ER staff slashed my sweater to find a mushy, mangled mess of road rash down my left side. They stacked a pyramid of thin, heated blankets around me and on top of me, but the warmth never went past my fingertips. I wedged my chattering jaw against the pillow and tried to answer the questions hurled from across the bed. *Do you know your name? Do you know where you are? Do you know what day it is? What were you doing in the road?* I leveraged answering their questions with my own about Jennie and Tara. No response. They jotted down the two names on the corner of my chart and promised to find out more.

An apologetic woman in green scrubs peeled the hospital gown from my left arm and removed a toothbrush from a plastic seal. She scrubbed at the raw remains of my shoulder, then dabbed at it with a white cloth. I felt it. Every stroke. I knew the tiny bits of gravel needed to come out, but the deeper she dug into the soft tissue, the more I shrunk back against the metal rails. "Helmet!" I solved the word puzzles on the game show out loud, only to notice the questioning looks of the nurses. I'm sure they wondered how hard I had hit my head.

The green scrubs lady slathered my left shoulder in Band-Aid-scented goop and wheeled me into an ominous room with a low table. I expected to see a dim light bulb hanging over an interrogator in suspenders, suit coat slung over the back of a chair. But in one smooth movement, faceless aides shifted my rigid body from the gurney onto the table. A seismic shift. As they twisted my arms and legs into perfect right-angle x-ray positions, I screamed—shrieks so guttural and unnatural I whimpered afterward, drool slipping from the corners of my mouth. The radiology tech walked out of the room as if nothing had happened, stopping only to wash his hands in a small sink.

While I waited to be wheeled out, I noticed that my right hand was swollen so large it looked like one of those medical gloves filled with air before you drew a chicken beak and feathers on it. I couldn't move my left leg or arm. I ran my tongue over the unfamiliar, newly jagged edges of my teeth, slicing the tip. It hit me like a Dodge Caravan going forty-five-plus miles per hour. *This is bad! I can't just walk it off.* It scared me to think that not one person had seen two other teenage girls in the ER.

· — ● — ·

I woke up right in the middle of the marathon surgery, a blue sheet walling off the white masks and metal trays weighed down with drills and screws. The large light fixture above me reflected a complete map of my broken body. Teams clustered around each limb. I saw my right wrist splayed open with a bunch of blue rubber gloves poking around inside. I suddenly had the prankster impulse to yank my hand away. Senseless, I know. In my head, I jerked my hand, but the reflection showed an inanimate limb, a Halloween prop seemingly severed from my body. I thought I saw my dad's motorcycle buddy, Scott, lean over to inspect my pupils before I drifted away again.

· — ● — ·

Chunky little toes peeked out from a brace, the big toe sporting an oxygen monitor clip. I wouldn't have noticed the clip, but its monitor screeched, tattling that my breathing wasn't up to par. Hyperventilating, I gulped huge gasps of air, trying to shut the thing off. After half a dozen tries, the nurse tossed it on the tray next to the bed and left. A couple of poles draped with color-coded tubes stood sentinel over my bedside, cords twisted, green numbers flickering. Pillows propped my legs up; my casted arms lay motionless against my sides. My bloated elbow throbbed, and I held it close. I pumped the button again for the nurse, hoping it was time for another dose of pain medication.

My mom stood up, her short brown hair tousled from a few minutes of sleep in the easy chair. She set her paperback on the table.

"Hey, how're you feeling? Need anything?" she whispered.

"How long have I been out?"

"You've been pretty much out of it for the last two days. They took you into surgery first thing this morning. It took most of the day." She rubbed her hands across her forehead. Her bright-green eyes were bloodshot, dark shadows underneath.

"What happened? When did you get to the hospital?"

She sighed. "Well after midnight. We didn't check the messages when we got home. We just got ready for bed."

"Then how did you know what happened?"

She shrugged. "It's funny, but Jake scratched at the front door to go potty. He wouldn't go out back."

I wished I could bear hug my fox-colored terrier, his black nose pressed against my chest. My throat tightened, and I nodded.

"Christensens left a sticky note on the front door to call them immediately." She looked out the window, the lines around her mouth drawn and deep.

"Are you okay?" I asked.

"I am. I just feel bad I wasn't there for you." She didn't turn around.

"But you were at the banquet. You came when you found out."

She pulled a stool up next to my bed and brushed my messy hair from my face. "I always thought I would know—you know?— that a mom would sense when her child was in trouble. And . . . I didn't. What kind of mom does that make me?"

"That says nothing about what kind of mom you are. I was in good hands, and the nurses said two aunts came. They didn't let them back into the ER, not that I saw. I think it was Joyce and Beth."

My mom stiffened slightly. "It should have been me. Can I get you anything?"

"Will you scratch the left side of my nose?" I turned my head, scrunching the bridge of my nose. Without functioning hands, I tried to gesture with my chin. "No, not there. Up a little. Down. There. Thanks. It's been bugging me."

"What have you been thinking about?" Mom asked.

"A little of everything. Track. Basketball. They were going to start me on Friday against Midvale. I don't know if I told you." I winced at the burning pain in my left ankle and frowned when I couldn't rotate the boot to get a better look at it.

"I know. When you came out of anesthesia, you kept asking if you had missed the game. We had to tell you every couple of minutes."

"Does Coach know?"

Mom shook her head. "I don't know."

"I've been sitting here wondering how this sets me back. You know, like, is this a hiccup and in six months I'll be back to normal, or will I ever run the same again?"

Her shoulders sagged, and her sad eyes met mine. "I don't know, Chani."

"What if I can't do anything again? What if I'm left looking like Frankenstein? Where do I go from here?" I smoothed my casts over the wrinkles in my hospital gown, not daring to look up. The pain in my leg throbbed now, working its way up to my knee. I inhaled through my nose and exhaled from my mouth, feeling the sweat bead on my forehead.

"Oh, I don't think it's like that. It's late. You're just tired. Try to get some sleep, and you'll feel better."

"I can't sleep. I've never been able to sleep on my back, and they wake me up every time they walk in the room."

Mom grinned her crooked smile and winked at me. "I'll watch for them." She stepped out into the hall and gently shut the door behind her.

I pressed my head against the pillow, thinking of my track mentor. Coach Hunter awarded green T-shirts to runners who pushed themselves so hard they lost their lunch in the big rusted barrel next to the supply shed—a symbol of sacrifice and determination. Although I'd cut carbonation out of my diet and read secondhand copies of *Runners Magazine* from the library, I never pushed myself that hard. Could I get back to where I once was? Would the scouts at the University of Utah still come to see me run? I knew they had seen potential in me. To give in was not my nature, but I could feel myself slowly deflating, not sure if I had enough determination to surpass a "Run till you chuck" T-shirt.

I didn't know who I was if I couldn't compete. But more than that, what was my purpose? What was the point? I sighed, staring at the four empty walls. A whiteboard adorned with my nurse's name and the last hour's stats taunted me. Was it worth the pain in my elbow to try to reach the TV button? I couldn't kneel. I couldn't put my hands together, but I bowed my head.

*Heavenly Father, I know it's been a long time since you've heard from me. I don't even know if you're there. I'm just lying here with nothing else to do, so we might as well catch up.*

*Heavenly Father, I'm confused. I've been to church almost every Sunday for my whole life. I'm not perfect, but I'm a good kid. Stuff like this happens to troublemakers. I follow the rules. I hang out with good friends, the kind who make me a better person. I keep honor-roll grades so I can get a scholarship. I don't know why this happened to me. Did I make a mistake?*

I reached down to rub my throbbing leg, and my cast smacked against the bed frame. I couldn't move my fingers, but I could press the weight of my arm against my leg and that was enough. I thought I heard the door creak open, and I cleared my throat. No one was there.

I remembered the last broken bone in our family. Without insurance, my dad's shattered wrist had left us without a paycheck for months and Mom had gone back to work to make ends meet. Our backyard neighbors gave us a deer from their last hunting trip. It fed our family. We couldn't afford much beyond that. I eyed the splints and casts and continued my prayer.

*I had a big argument with Mom and Dad a few weeks ago about not playing basketball because they couldn't afford the fees. They told Coach, and he worked it out with them. Our family struggles as it is. I'm not stupid. I don't know how much an ambulance ride costs, but a night in the hospital could ruin my family. Mom doesn't know what to do. I see it in her eyes. I feel so guilty.*

*I've been awake for a while; I just didn't want to face my family yet. I told Mom I was worried about sports. And I am, but I couldn't tell her the rest. I mean, for reals, why didn't you . . . take me? Why did you let me live? Am I worth it? Really?*

*Mom should be home tonight with Marie and Nick. They're probably really scared. I am. I know I shouldn't be, but I sit here picturing my family's life without me. They would be sad for a while, but they would move on. I couldn't tell Mom I was thinking that.*

*I don't want to be a lifelong burden to them. I wish I would have just passed away quickly. I know that sounds dramatic. If there's something I can do to change it—but I can't. I can't do that to Mom and Dad. But I don't want to sink them either. You might think I'm horrible for saying that. I'm sorry. I just don't know what to do.*

*I feel weird even talking to you when it's been so long. You're probably not even listening to me anyway. Never mind. Um . . . amen.*

## Questions for the Reader:

*Have you ever felt distant from God?*

*Do you believe He is really there?*

*Have you ever wondered about the purpose of YOUR life?*

# The Lucky One

In the hallway, the cadence of muffled voices rose and fell next to Dorothy's nurse station. I heard the bellowing, gusty laugh that made her whole body shake, and I smiled. I bet my parents had stopped at Banbury Cross Bakery and brought her a hot cinnamon-crumble doughnut. It was their cure for everything. Someone tapped on the oversized hospital door, and it swung open like a revolving mall entrance. My dad walked in wearing a navy-blue windbreaker zipped up to his neck, his gray trucker hat balanced on top of his sandy hair. My mom flanked the walls, arms folded across her chest.

A gentleman in a starched lab coat tiptoed to the side of my bed. From the proper way he stood, he could have removed a top hat and draped a white linen cloth over his forearm as he introduced himself. Instead, he pulled the rolling stool up next to me and sat, ramrod straight, evaluating me with piercing blue eyes. "You're awake. That's promising." He rolled a few inches closer. "Chantelle, I'm Dr. Leslie Harris. It's nice to finally meet you. You're a lucky little lady, you know that?"

I mumbled something he took as agreement. I tried to turn my head to better meet his gaze, but the thick layer of tape along my neck and jaw prevented it.

"Oh, I'm sorry. This tape is to hold your IV in place. We had to put it in your neck because, well, there just wasn't anywhere else to put it." He gestured to my broken body and chuckled breathily. He seemed to be sucking in air. If only he knew what I was thinking.

He looked up at my parents. "I was actually supposed to be in Park City this weekend. I'm a traveling specialist. I'm only at this hospital once or twice a month and rarely on weekends. It's a good thing I was here. I was the head of the surgical team and coordinated all the different orthopedic specialists."

Dad cracked a joke I couldn't quite hear, and Dr. Harris chuckled a couple more times. I'm sure it was a pun on "head," something about having his head on straight or not losing his head. I bet you were head of the class. So predictable. My mom grinned, rolled her eyes, and slid into the brown recliner. She tilted her good ear toward us, head propped on her arm. No one would ever know she was deaf on one side. She hid it so well.

"Well, let's get down to business." Dr. Harris put his foot on the edge of the stool and locked his fingers together in his lap. He looked directly at me, unblinking. "You have experienced several fractures, abrasions, and ligament tears. Let's just start at the top of the list and make our way down." He pointed at my elbow with a fancy black pen, the kind that comes in a velvet case. "Your left humerus was fractured and required a small pin to repair it. We had to make an incision about four inches long." He shifted the pen. "Your left wrist was fractured, but it was a clean break and did not require surgical intervention. We just braced it." The pen bobbed in his hand, pointing to the heavy wrapping around my hand. "I'm sure you noticed your right wrist. We performed a carpal tunnel release almost immediately to relieve the swelling there. We basically had to reconstruct your right hand and wrist. You have a plate with several screws and pins holding it in place. Be careful with it. As the swelling goes down, we will need to recast."

I groaned. *Shoot.* My right hand was my lifeline. I had never been anything close to ambidextrous. My left hand only assisted in buttoning my jeans and making my body look symmetrical.

Anytime I attempted a left-handed layup, Coach shook his head and exhaled a puff of air. He finally gave up and told me to just use my right hand. I flexed the swollen tips of the fingers poking out of the cast and realized Dr. Harris's shiny pen had moved down the list.

"... femur required two large screws. You have a torn posterior cruciate ligament (PCL) in the right knee." He formed an X with his index fingers and indicating which part of the X was my PCL. "We will wait and see how everything else mends before we address it. For now, it will feel loose and may give out.

"Your left ankle was the worst. Your calcaneus, or heel, was completely crushed. We had to reconstruct your entire ankle with plates, screws, and pins. Let's just say you might set off a few metal detectors for a while." Again, he breathily sucked in air, chuckling to himself. No one else joined him. He paused. "I know that's a lot all at once. Do you have any questions?"

I didn't want to ask, but I wanted a real, honest answer, however painful. For years, I had practiced the national anthem so that when I finally stood on the podium, cameras flashing, with the weight of an Olympic medal around my neck, I would know all the words. I knew it would happen. That was the *me* before the accident. My fresh concept of *me* seemed iffy. With broken teeth and rugged, raw scars, my mirror image plummeted from average to freakishly horrific. I couldn't meet Dr. Harris's eyes. My question bubbled to the surface as he waited patiently. I swallowed against my dry mouth, attempted to moisten my lips, and whispered, "Will I ever play sports again?"

He hesitated, and then his eyes softened. He stole a serious look at my parents, then leaned forward, his blue eyes level with mine. "How about we focus on walking? It's going to take some time to get you walking first. Then we'll look a little further ahead." He straightened, nodding at my mom. I wasn't sure what that meant. Then he stood to leave, his shiny, tasseled loafers poking out from under his neatly pressed trousers. He paused at the door and ran his hand through his hair. I don't know how his practiced surgical fingers avoided disheveling his short, wavy locks, but they didn't move at all.

"You know, to be honest, I'm completely puzzled by your injuries. I can understand the damage to your arms and hands by the nature of the impact, but I have no idea how your legs sustained the injuries they did or how you avoided any internal damage. Your organs and spine are all completely unharmed. You don't even appear to have signs of a concussion." He bit his lip and gestured to the charts in the room. "I'm not a forensic expert, but with the speed the driver reported, the size of the van, and the fact that you were hit directly, you really shouldn't have . . . Well, you really are a very lucky little lady."

I nodded, feeling the tape pull at my neck, a few strands of my hair caught in it. He left the room, and my parents followed. A nurse toted a hospital thermos into the room. She defaced it with "NO ICE" in permanent marker and set it down next to me. *No way. Not again.* I knew they'd told me I needed to stay hydrated, but I cringed at the thought of cold water on the exposed nerves in my teeth. I'd rather have my fingernails torn out one by one.

I ignored the thermos and chewed the inside of my cheek, replaying the conversation with Dr. Harris in my head. Each time I heard my own pitiful question, *Will I ever play sports again?* I simmered even more, and my mood dipped. Dr. Harris, a specialist, a professional among professionals, couldn't answer me. Though he probably didn't realize it, his hesitance had smashed my waning hope. I absorbed the blow and folded inside myself. I thought about praying again, but it was pointless. If God could hear me, what could He do? Reverse time? I wasn't sure I wanted Him to overhear the choice words percolating in my mind.

I knew I should be grateful. Grateful to be alive. Grateful for the Madrigal Choir that came and sang Christmas carols to a solo audience member. Grateful my entire basketball team stopped by after practice. They crept near my hospital bed, but not one teammate looked up at me. They stared at their matching blue-and-white high-tops and poked the orange fluid bags hanging precariously beside me. I clenched my teeth. I was a burden.

For a brief moment, relief enveloped me when Mrs. Simper called my parents to let them know Jennie had been hit but was okay. She had been life-flighted to another hospital and released the next day without a single stitch or broken bone. Apparently, Tara made it across the road unscathed. I was the "lucky" one.

The get-well cards collected in haphazard piles around the room, but I didn't pick them up. Not then, at least. Family members, friends, and neighbors knocked timidly on the door. I couldn't form the words to invite them in. I took long, deep breaths, feeling a new pain so acute it didn't register on the nurses' whiteboard stats. It was easier to pretend to sleep. I knew they were there, every one of them, but I didn't have the strength to face them. I felt I was already a ball and chain to those I loved. A financial strain. I didn't want their pity too.

Around the clock, the nurses documented my slippery depression. Two days later, on December 6, after a volunteer placed my half-eaten breakfast tray in the hallway, she brought in a small cupcake with an unlit candle. I barely raised my head, mustering a weak smile. "Happy sweet sixteen." Dorothy ceremoniously removed the IV from my neck and the catheter (by far the best birthday present I have ever been given). I nearly cried when Gidget the nurse offered to shave under my arms and wash away the orange-and-brown smears left over from surgery prep. She braided my greasy hair, and I felt a little more human, less of a spectacle. Every visitor brought a slice of cake that day, whether they saw me or not. Humbled, I offered the extra to the rooms down the hall. We probably fed the entire east wing with white sponge cake.

At one point, one of the members of my church congregation brought a wrapped gift. I'd received cards and flowers, but this was the first gift. Intrigued, I rubbed my cast over the shiny Christmas paper, slipping the tips of my fettered fingers under the Scotch tape. On a day when I should be celebrating a milestone birthday with friends and dipping salty chips in salsa, I sat upright in a hospital bed resenting the Santa Clause movie on TV and the consolation prize in my hand. I uncovered a cardboard backing and allowed the paper to flutter to the floor beside the hospital bed. I turned it over to discover a painting of Jesus Christ.

It wasn't new. I had seen the picture held up in nursery and primary children's classes since I could wear tights. It hung on the textured walls of my high school scripture-study class. Taking in the off-white mat and plastic seal, I read the calligraphic caption. "I never said it would be easy; I only said it would be worth it." I could have launched it across the room, growling, "You have no idea. I am nobody. I am nothing. Because of all this, there is nothing special about me anymore." But for some reason, I didn't throw it.

Instead, I rested the picture on my lap, ignoring the bottle of chocolate Ensure on my folding tray. I traced the letters, avoiding the earnest eyes of the Savior. "I never said it would be easy . . ." I turned it facedown and jammed it under my pillows. I considered the message throughout the afternoon. Maybe it was the setting. Maybe it was because I was alone, my self-worth profoundly in question. But after visiting hours, I retrieved the picture and summoned the courage to look at His face. But something was different when I observed the picture this time. More personal. For the first time since opening my eyes to the blood on the pavement, I made room for the possibility that someone else, somewhere else, had experienced an overwhelmingly arduous path.

"I never said it would be easy; I only said it would be worth it." I didn't experience a Hallelujah chorus or Grinch-worthy instant change of heart, but I felt peace. For a brief moment, it consoled me in a way nothing else had. It was as if God Himself had entered my hospital room, winked at my pretend sleep, penetrated my wall of bitterness, and put His arms around me, careful not to jostle the pillow stacks. *Chani, this will be hard but worth it. You're worth it.*

I wasn't a crier. In fact, I had entered my double-digit years without shedding a tear. I prided myself on the dry streak, convinced I could avoid the label "emotional teenage girl" if I didn't cry at all. But now the dam burst. Years of pent-up emotion surged through my stoic facade. I sobbed for my broken body. I mourned the life I would now live, the accolades that would never come. I finally let myself feel it all.

The newspapers covered my story, but I wasn't headline-worthy. I was a little blip a couple of inches tall, a side note in the local section. It talked about my splintered hips, my fractured back, and my critical condition. Thankfully, things were never that bleak. I picked up a stack of cards from my brother's fourth-grade class and actually chuckled at the gruesome renderings of a person being mauled by a car. The captions read, "I'm glad you're not dead" and "Watch out next time." My driver's ed teacher got a belly laugh for the packet on pedestrian safety he sent me. I had to circle all the pictures of pedestrians not obeying traffic laws to get full credit.

The day a rumpled, unshaven man in a plaid shirt thundered into my hospital room unannounced was a defining moment. The tags on his lanyard introduced him as Bill, a physical therapist, but the toolbox in his other hand and the pencil over his ear suggested otherwise. Bill fashioned a makeshift walker so I could push forward with my right elbow and hop on my not-as-bad right leg. I protested as he lashed a harness to my hips and pulled me to a standing position. I couldn't do it.

As I put my full weight on my legs, fire surged through my joints. I whimpered, trying to sit back down, but my body buckled, and I barely caught the edge of the bed to cushion my fall.

"You're not even trying!" he accused. He pulled on my harness again, not even bothering to offer a steadying hand.

I felt the fire again, but not in my swollen limbs. A slow, red-hot anger ignited in my chest and flared my nostrils. *I am trying, you jerk! Bet you couldn't do it. You have no idea who you're messing with!* I bit my lip against the searing pain and took a small step. One measly hop. I never earned Bill's praise, but he nodded and carted his toolbox out of the room.

It wasn't about my first sloppy step. Bill had tapped into a fiery determination that never snuffed out. "I can't" melted into "Watch out!" That gritty alteration proved to be one of the most meaningful steps I have ever taken.

• — ● — •

My family loaded the large, not-so-user-friendly wheelchair into the back of our Toyota minivan, its seats removed. I ducked to avoid the lip of the back door as they tipped me up a wooden ramp and inside. My dad's motorcycle ratchet tie-downs secured my wheels in place and anchored me to the inside of the van. It took a handful of neighbors to carry me up the front steps of my house and push me inside. My daybed sat against the living room wall, a cheerful Christmas tree in the corner.

I stayed up well after bedtime many nights, staring at the warm lights of the Christmas tree in that shadowed room. My dog always slept on my bed, nuzzled against my healing body, one paw on my arm. I thought a lot about the coincidences from the accident. Each by itself seemed insignificant, but put together, I saw tiny miracles piling up. My last-minute action of lifting my hands to brace for impact had saved my life. The orthopedic surgeon who was supposed to be elsewhere that night being the only one with the skill set to handle my injuries. The dog going out the front door to pee. My aunts stepping in when my parents could not be reached. My accident bridged gaps between grudge-holding siblings, original offenses long since forgotten. I eventually met the woman driving the car and was able to piece together the explanations for my unique injuries and those moments I couldn't remember clearly.

I began to recognize that I was never alone. Someone had known my name while I was lying on the ground under a Mario sleeping bag. Someone had told me to stay still while the crew loaded Jennie into the helicopter. That person met with my parents days later in the hospital. They wanted to reassure them someone had held my hand when they couldn't be there. But more than that, someone had watched over me. Call it God. Call it a guardian angel. To this day, divine intervention is the only possible explanation for why I survived. I still don't know why some accidents end in tragedy and mine didn't. I don't take it lightly. I figure God still has something He needs me to do.

## Questions for the Reader:

*Have you considered that the coincidences in your life might be evidence that God is aware of you?*

*Have you ever had an experience where you felt close to God?*

# I Hate Waiting

My dad's jingling keys and scrunched-up nose always meant "Grab your coat and find your shoes now! I don't care if you have to pee. Go get in the car."

My maternal grandma used to rap her knuckles hard on the table after each turn at cards. If I took too much time to decide between spades or hearts, her gnarled hand thumped again, a little closer and a lot harder.

Let's just say the patience gene had failed to thrive on either side of my family. The physical therapists patted my shoulder for years, assuring me that some things just took time. I loathed that advice. As I stretched the large orange rubber bands behind my knees and around my ankles, I grumbled about my slow progress. I snuck a little more weight resistance onto the machines, hoping to heal on my own timeframe. By the time I donned a blue cap and gown, I walked confidently to the podium to receive my high school diploma without a limp. Coach Hunter spotlighted me at the awards banquet, with tears in his eyes, as one of the most tenacious track captains he had ever coached.

In my personal relationships, however, I simply couldn't alter the timeline. I graduated high school without ever having been kissed. Most guys invited me over as the fifth member of their street basketball games. They whacked my back when I hit an outside three or stole the ball from the lumbering forward, but they never looked my in direction when considering dates for Friday night.

But I knew. Someday a man would offer me his arm and open my door like in the black-and-white movies. He would be a spiritual man, a man close to God. He would hover somewhere around six feet tall, play the piano, and throw a solid fastball. He would lean on his elbow over a candlelit table, so intensely focused on my eyes his sleeve might end up in his mashed potatoes. He'd write me notes to let me know he couldn't stop thinking about me and tape them to my windshield, next to my fuzzy red dice.

I thought of him as I drove up Sunnyside Avenue to the University of Utah one morning and parked my yellow Sunbird in the north parking lot. When my classes ended for the day, I snatched a peanut butter only on white and managed the night shift at a local bookstore.

"Kurt, will you bring me that box of CDs?" I asked another employee from across the room.

The tall man in a crisp white shirt grabbed the box with one hand and set it on the floor. "Oh, um, it's Keith. Keith Barlow."

I flinched as the patient, a late addition to our holiday help, reached into the box and handed me a stack to inventory. My cheeks flushed, and I grumbled to myself. *Keith. Not Kurt. Keith.*

I filled a rolling cart with the contents of the boxes and told the new guy to find spots on the shelves for the shipment. I didn't look twice. To be fair, the last guy we'd hired used everything on the displays as lightsabers. I'd kept a safe distance.

But every holiday season ends. We removed the white Christmas lights from the window display and stopped rotating the holiday classics over the sound system. Overtime hours gave way to a more predictable pattern. We marked down the overstock and waited for someone to enter our retail shop for something other than a gift return. For the first time since Autumn, we caught our breath and paused.

In January 2000, I began to notice tall, easygoing, blue-eyed Keith. He could rattle off all the BYU quarterbacks since the mid-

'60s in order and mimic Harry Caray calling Cubs' games on WGN. He could name obscure Alfred Hitchcock movies, quote *Seven Brides for Seven Brothers* in casual conversation, and convert any tune into a big-band number like Dean Martin. Like me, he probably belonged in a different decade. Intrigued, I asked him out.

Our first date almost didn't happen. Someone got sick at work and left us shorthanded. One of us had to cover an extra shift and close up the store. Even with the lights dimmed and the door locked, customers shopped well past closing time that night. We considered rescheduling, but we ultimately decided on a dive-y deli with a neon "Open until Midnight" sign peeking out the solitary window.

I wore an impressive yellow track T-shirt and pair of warm-ups, a test to see if he accepted the authentic me. I didn't play games. He borrowed his brother's black truck, and we fiddled with the complex stubborn face of the car stereo, much too complex to turn on. Instead, we talked. We placed our order with a worker behind a deep counter and carried our trays to a sticky table with cracked blue seat covers.

Keith covered his scone sandwich with more mustard than I had eaten in a lifetime and squashed the top back on. I nervously picked at my spicy fries, blowing on them before taking a bite. "What made you think of working at the bookstore?" I asked.

He shrugged. "I was actually working as a missionary in England up until July and needed extra cash for Christmas. I'm the oldest in a big family."

"I'm from a big family too. I've lost count of all my cousins. Where in England?"

"Bristol, mostly. I served in the south part of England and Wales."

It nudged at my heart. I wondered if I would make a good missionary and still turned it over in my head as a possibility. "Did your family ever give you a hard time about being a missionary? I thought I heard you were a convert," I said.

Keith set his sandwich down and looked at me directly. "My extended family, yes. But my parents have always been there for me, even when I chose to serve a mission. Their beliefs aren't quite like mine, but they raised me to read the scriptures. They taught me about God. They provided the foundation for the faith I have now. Leaving them for two years was the hardest thing I've ever done. I'm a homebody. We are a big family, but we're very close."

"Was it nice to be home with them for Christmas?" I stole a glance at the employee wandering from table to table with a wet rag and spray bottle.

"Oh yeah. My mom is one of those people who plays Christmas music in August. She sets up the tree as soon as possible." His eyes shone. "Don't get me wrong. Nothing beats Christmastime in England, but it was good to be back. What about you? What did you do for Christmas?"

"We mostly stayed here. My grandparents came to visit. I'm still getting used to it, actually. They never used to visit us during the holidays. We always came to them. I don't think my grandma left home during Christmas until a few years ago."

"What changed?" Keith leaned forward, balling up his sandwich wrapper.

"That was the year of my accident, the year I was hit by a car."

"You were hit by a car?" He raised his eyebrows and opened his lid to stir another lemon into his soda.

"I know how it sounds. Yeah, I was jaywalking right here on Redwood Road with a couple of friends." I could probably point out the intersection if I stood up next to the neon sign.

"How bad were you hurt?"

"Pretty bad." I turned my wrist over, revealing the ugly red scar there. I yanked up my warm-ups to show my knee and pulled down my sock around a misshapen, blotchy ankle with a scar pulling the skin too tight. Keith winced as I pointed to each.

"Do they still bother you?" he asked.

"Sometimes. My legs still give out, but I can run again. Not competitively, but I can run. I just can't hike. I completely lost the sideways motion in my foot and some feeling in my knee."

"Wow. I can't imagine how hard that must have been."

I nodded. "It really was, but I was blessed. In fact, I can honestly say that if I could go back and change things, I don't know that I would." I looked down at my track pants and rubbed at my knee, even though it didn't ache.

"Really? Why is that?"

"Our family is closer because of it. I've seen miracles happen as a result."

"Miracles? Like what?"

"Well, in me, to start. Everyone worked so hard to save my life and fix my body—I wasn't sure if I was worth all that effort. Pretty low point for me. But even in that dark place, I felt like God was there with me."

"That's incredible," Keith whispered.

"It wasn't that I didn't believe in God before then. I just figured He had too much going on to worry about the details of my life. But that's not true." I blushed, knowing my voice was much louder than I intended. "You know, I reach out to Him with every little step toward recovery. He's there every time. My faith is solid. Because of what I've been through with my accident, I know I can trust Him with whatever life throws at me. Even if I have a few scars." I straightened my elbow, displaying a purple, L-shaped ridge. After a brief pause, I chided myself for saying too much. This was a first date!

"If it makes you feel any better, I was in an accident too. That's where I got this." He pointed to a waxy, white scar on the side of his nose. It stretched to his cheek.

I had noticed it before but never asked.

"Bike accident. I was riding on the handlebars when we hit a rock. I don't remember a thing. The scar's less visible than it used to be."

"Mine have yet to go down," I admitted. "I'm proud of them, though. I worked really hard to rehab every one of my injuries."

"You should be proud! That took a lot of patience. The doctors offered me plastic surgery to take care of my scars."

"And what happened?"

He shrugged and stretched his back. "I knew my parents couldn't afford it."

"Has it been hard on you to have a scar on your face, you know, front and center?" I asked, trying not to appear too curious.

"When I was on my mission, a cab driver turned and looked at me. The British are blunt. He pointed at my face and said, 'You know, that spoils your good looks.' Things like that sting, but most days, I don't even think about it."

I looked at the man sitting across from me, his arm draped over the back of the bench. I could see the love he had for his family but could feel the hurt from who knows how many thoughtless comments had been thrown his way. I lifted a few locks of hair near my hairline. "I'm not sure why the scar on my forehead turned blue. People are always trying to tactfully point out that I have ink on my head. It's funny, really, and not very attractive."

"It's all in how you look at them. I think they're attractive. I don't know how you handled it. It makes me want to know more about you," he confessed.

As my cheeks warmed under his gaze, I took my cup in my hands and shook the ice around before taking another sip.

The more I talked with Keith, the more I wanted to talk with him. His quirky sarcasm and puns rivaled only my dad's. We discovered our families had always lived within five minutes of each other. I'd probably roller-skated past his house or stood on his doorstep at Halloween. If we hadn't met at work, we would have filled our cars at the same gas station. As I wiped my windows clean, he might have offered to get the spots I'd missed at the top. I would have sauntered inside and surprised him with a soft-serve ice cream cone. We probably would have eaten them on the only grassy patch in the parking lot in front of everyone. It might have happened.

I couldn't wait to see him again. Keith and I talked for hours one day in the bookstore break room, sharing a sesame chicken and pot-stickers lunch on unopened inventory boxes. In the evening, we trekked to the ice arena, our hands magnetically woven together. I couldn't tell you when the puck dropped or when the final whistle blew. When pressed, I'll admit I knew after only two weeks of spending every waking hour with Keith that I wanted to spend forever with him. I hate waiting.

Keith teased me that in Wales, Leap Year Day was the only day a woman could propose to a man. I laughed it off. He mentioned it when we passed jewelry store windows. He dropped the hint again when I wrote him a Valentine's poem about saving my kisses for him. *He really wants me to ask?* Flustered, I couldn't recall a single classic film where a strong, leading lady tucked a gold band into her muff and proposed to Cary Grant over Olive Garden breadsticks. That's just not how I pictured it.

On February 29, Keith set up a group date for us with a couple of his cousins. I stopped at 7-11 on the way to his house, thinking I might joke my way through the proposal. I eyed the watermelon ring pop, the best flavor. My fingers drummed nervously against my slacks, considering. *No. I can't do it. Not in front of people I've never met.* I pushed out the door and rested my hands on the steering wheel before putting the key in the ignition. I looked at my reflection in the rearview mirror. I wanted to ask him. I really did. I shifted the mirror away from my panic-stricken expression.

At dinner, I shook hands with Liam and Joel Lucas and chatted with Brooke and Alisa about how they'd first met each other. I hoped none of them picked up on the shakiness of my voice or my shy, somewhat petrified smile. Keith placed his arm protectively around my shoulder and squeezed it. He nodded encouragement. I took a deep breath and sat up straight, wanting him to know that his confidence in me was not misplaced.

Our conversation stuck primarily to safe, superficial topics, and I gleaned a little insight into Keith as a teenager. We breezed through our salads without an awkward pause. I appreciated that. I thought I was out of the woods by the time I'd downed my last few bites of fettuccine.

"So, when are you guys going to get married already?" Liam prodded as he tossed his napkin onto his cleared plate.

I looked up, straining to swallow the noodle in my throat. I tipped my water glass to my lips. He couldn't have known about Leap Year in Wales or the watermelon ring pop I hadn't bought. I didn't know what to say. My cheeks burned, my eyes pleading for a diversion from the one man who ever saw me as beautiful.

"I guess we'll just have to see how things go," Keith said, placing his fork on his plate. He winked at me. Or maybe I just thought he did in the dimmed room. I couldn't be sure.

Our waitress left us a check with a smiley face hastily drawn on the front. She placed a small tray of mints on the table and stood aside while we zipped our coats. She was ready for us to be done and call it a night. So was I.

Keith opened my car door, hummed life into the freezing engine, rounded 7th East, and pulled into Murray Park. We walked the unlit trail, my fingers clasped in his warm hands, until we reached a bridge and paused.

"What do you think about what Liam said tonight?"

"About getting married?"

I nodded in the dark.

He pulled me close, leaning up against the guardrail on the bridge. He brushed his lips against the top of my head, his breath visible. I rested my head against his chest, close enough to feel his thrumming heartbeat.

He chuckled out loud. "Do you know what I just remembered? You haven't met my family during football season. It's pretty intense. Do you think you could put up with something like that?"

I backed away from his bear hug, grinning. "That's nothing. Fair warning: When I play card games, I play to win. I take no responsibility for what comes out of my mouth when I lose."

"I think I'll take my chances."

I looked up at him, his face shadowed by the trees. "Does this mean we're getting married?"

"I guess so. Yeah."

I sifted through my tiny treasure chest the minute I walked through my bedroom door. I pulled out a dollar-store rhinestone ring and slid it on my left hand as a placeholder. Three weeks later, Keith led me to the very same spot on the park trail, on the exact bridge, this time in the daylight. He pulled a silver gift box from behind his back and handed it to me. I opened it, shoving aside the white tissue paper to find an intricately carved wooden spoon.

"This is a Welsh love spoon," he explained, taking it in his hands and tracing the carvings. He didn't look up. "In Wales, it is tradition for a man to give it to the woman he wants to marry. The carvings are symbolic. The hearts are for eternal love. The horseshoes are for good luck. I saw it years ago and bought it, knowing I would one day find someone. I've been waiting." He paused, looking directly into my eyes. "And now I want to give it to you."

Touched, I took the spoon from him, turning it over. I thought of the nights I prayed for this man, the one who saw through my tough exterior and loved all of me. My best friend. Maybe he'd prayed for me too. He might not have known my name, but he knew we would find each other. He trusted that. I'm not sure there is a classic movie out there that can duplicate that kind of romance.

He reached into his pocket, then slung his black leather jacket over the post of the guardrail. I expected his usual container of Carmex, but he pulled out a black velvet box instead and dropped to his knee. Since I knew it was coming, I didn't burst into tears. I didn't gasp with my hands flying to my mouth. I knelt in front of him and held him so long we somehow lost the jacket in the middle of all the excitement. It might have fallen in the water while we kissed. We never did find it.

We were married six months after our first date. We served chocolate ice cream and hazelnut cookies at our reception. I proudly sported white sneakers under my dress and a Nike swish on my wedding cake. Later that night, we muted *Monty Python and the Holy Grail* and dubbed our own voices and commentary.

When Keith laughs, really laughs, his eyes flood with tears and he barely squeaks out a high-pitched giggle he covers with his long fingers. I kissed him after every squeak.

We rented a little shoebox apartment in Salt Lake City off of 78th and State, filling it with clashing hand-me-down furniture from various decades. I bought a small oak table and four chairs at a going-out-of-business sale. Every time I sat at that table, I thought proudly, *I only spent ninety-nine dollars for this whole set.* We discussed a lot at that table. Mayo or Miracle Whip? Butter or margarine? Sandwiches cut horizontally or diagonally? But more importantly—start our family now or focus on school?

Keith, in his retro Cubs T-shirt, camped out on the start-our-family-now side. I wasn't surprised. I could picture him diving through sprinklers, his blonde pompadour flat against his forehead, his Chuck Taylors soaked through. I knew he looked forward to digging in the dirt with kitchen spoons right alongside our little ones.

For me, all my girl-power ideas let loose. I shunned the vision of a baby on my hip. I pictured my textbook on the table drizzled with baby formula and mediocre test scores. I didn't want it. It wasn't fair to bring a little one into the picture when we could barely care for ourselves. With all these massive life decisions plowing toward me, I turned to the only path to truth I knew—prayer.

And God answered. Oh, boy, did He answer.

## Questions for the Reader:

*How do you approach major life decisions?*

*Who is your truest friend, the friend you can count on no matter what?*

# This Was Different

My dad hoarded boxes of ice cream sandwiches in the freezer for anyone who passed our driveway. My mom constructed a magic fairy garden in a flowerpot just to see little children crouch in front in front of it, their fingers itching to touch the enchanting little world. But my parents' love for others pales in comparison to the love they have for God. They involve Him in their marriage and major life decisions.

When Keith and I veered in opposite directions on when to start our family, I followed my parents' example. Keith and I knelt together. With my hand enveloped in his, we poured out our questions and confusion for weeks, side by side. I knew God would answer me, but I didn't know how.

One night, I hugged my pillow next to my cheek and sighed, submitting to sleep after a long day in the billing office waiting on hold with insurance companies and debating coinsurance amounts and deductibles. I eased one leg under the blankets, one leg out, my MO on any given night. But something was different that night. My eyes closed quickly, and I felt the tension slip off my shoulders and neck. My breathing aligned with Keith's, and I drifted off to sleep.

In my mind, I stood at the sink in a kitchen flooded with sunlight. I didn't recognize the light cabinets or windows around me. A busy little toddler ambled near me, the warm rays of sun caressing his back, accenting the highlights in his blond hair and full cheeks. He played with a ball. He stopped and grinned at me. Breakfast dribbles spattered the front of his white-and-blue-striped shirt. The moment paused. I didn't dare move.

His earnest eyes begged for my attention. I stared at him but wasn't sure why. The more I looked at him, the more I knew it. He knew me. He needed me. I swallowed away the urge to cry out and throw my arms around his little body. No words were necessary. I was going to be a mom. We were going to have a son!

I rolled onto my back, eyes wide open. The snapshot was imprinted so distinctly on each of my senses I could still feel the soapy water in the sink. I could hear the ball cracking against the chair's wooden legs as he chased it. His innocent face was stamped permanently into my thoughts. More than that, an indescribable feeling of love and peace permeated my heart. I whispered my gratitude to God, tears trickling sideways through my hair and onto the checkered sheets.

Keith was no stranger to my quirky dreams. He'd endured the harrowing details of my close calls with mob bosses and car chases. He'd ignored my warnings that a spy had entrapped his family. But this dream was different. I shook him awake, and he lazily lifted his arm so I could curl up against his chest. I told him everything. He slurred his tired agreement at first but then absorbed each of my words, one at a time. He sat up in bed and threw his legs over the side.

After such a powerful vision and its companion feeling of peace, I didn't need to stop and analyze for too long. Unified, Keith and I trusted that God knew our situation better than we did. A little boy waited on the sidelines; I was certain. We didn't need to wait for financial stability, a degree, or an established career before welcoming him into our home.

I thought I would become pregnant right away. It seemed so easy for everyone else. As the months passed, the bellies around us began to swell: those of family members, neighbors, friends. At church, every woman's lap either had a maternity shirt stretched over her protruding belly or a newborn on it. Not mine. My empty lap stood out as if under an uncomfortable spotlight. Older ladies tapped my shoulder, wondering if I had any announcements to share. I shamefully shook my head. At baby showers, I retreated to the snack table, nibbling at sandwiches, unable to contribute to the embellished birth stories shared.

At the doctor's insistence, I began taking my temperature and tracking my daily statistics. Was I ovulating? Was I regular? Was anything off? I filled out the charts with shaking pen, diligently at first, then less so as the months crawled on. None of the blood or urine tests indicated a problem. Still, the memory of my little boy assured me I would be a mom someday. I held on to that. I needed it. It allowed me to hold my head high and bite back my snarky retorts when others accused me of being selfish for not wanting children.

I clung to that snapshot as a nurse with a butterfly tattoo strapped my legs to a gynecological exam chair, my feet high in the air. Keith turned his bloodless face away as the specialist injected toxic dye into my abdomen. The monitors squawked. My stomach repelled the foreign liquid and I dry heaved to the side. We both wobbled out the door, hoping for the relief only a clear answer could provide. If we could diagnose the problem, we could find a solution.

• — ● — •

I received the phone call at my billing office desk. I could picture Dr. Forrester with her scraggly, graying hair and oversized glasses lifting her chin as she perused a clipboard just inches from her face. Her monotone voice informed me that the dye test indicated a problem. Because of an anatomical abnormality, likely present since birth, we could not conceive a child. Pregnancy for me was dangerously high-risk, with only a smidgen of a chance at success. I floundered with how to respond, stuttering into the phone, nodding like a bobblehead doll. I had failed my husband. It was all my fault. The computer screen blurred in front of me, and I swiped at my runny nose.

Dr. Forrester cleared her throat and shuffled the papers on her clipboard, which also revealed the clinical reality of Keith's flatlined test results. Between the two of us lay a damning double dose of infertility. It wasn't funny. I wished she could have seen my bottom lip quiver. Maybe if I sat in her office, she would have burst through her crusty professional shell and taken me in her arms. She might have hugged me, telling me this wasn't the end. I was so young. But I wasn't in the office. I was a voice on the phone. A nobody. Mechanically, she wished me a nice day.

I thanked her and excused myself to the break room—a long, skinny space with a small fridge and a sink at the far end, a telephone balanced between the two. I traced the specks on the white Formica countertop, ignoring the smell of Hot Pockets and Lean Cuisine leftovers wafting from the microwave, then picked up the receiver and dialed my sister. I couldn't talk to Keith—not yet.

Marie answered, but I apologized immediately and hung up, collapsing onto the plastic folding table, my shoulders shuddering and every other part of my body leaking, sweating, or dripping with tears. I have no idea how my coworkers found me there. Nancy got my purse from the drawer and retrieved my car keys. I don't remember being sent home or the twenty-minute drive.

I checked my face in the rearview mirror, patting the small red blotches near my puffy eyes. I fumbled with our apartment door and found it unlocked. Surprised to see me, Keith turned away from his homework at the table, a Thompson Twins song droning on in the background. I steadied my breathing, but he saw it. He didn't have to ask.

I dropped my purse in the doorway, car keys and Chapstick rolling out onto the linoleum. I crumpled into his arms, no longer strong enough to shoulder the results alone. Our legs buckled, and we leaned into the kitchen cabinets, nearly spilling the dog dishes.

"Dr. Forrester called me," I confessed.

"Not good news?"

"No, not good news." I felt fresh pain inside my throat, and I covered my mouth with my hand. I didn't know where to start. I couldn't form the words. But I needed him to know. He deserved that much. In defeat, I explained our test results while rubbing the scar on the palm of my right hand.

He buried his head in my shoulder, his breath caught in his throat, his body trembling. I stroked his face and the soft spot on his neck I had kissed a million times. I had never seen him cry. I could only hold him and let our tears run dry together. When the sobbing ceased and our heads ached, we sat in silence, watching the noonday shadows of the tree outside the window. It rustled back and forth like a nosy neighbor trying to get a better view of us to gossip about tonight after dark.

Keith stood and pulled me to my feet. "Let's go out," he suggested.

"We just paid tuition. We don't have the money to go out. Not even a dollar menu. Not right now."

"I don't care. We are going to look back on this day for our whole lives. I want happy memories to go along with it. Come on. I want to take you out."

"Give me a minute." I dashed to the bedroom, anxious to shed my sweltering fuzzy sweater. I shoved it to the bottom of the hamper, covering it with all the other clothes. I never wore it again.

I ordered penne with pink sauce and dipped torn pieces of rustic rosemary bread in olive oil and balsamic vinegar. We doodled with crayons on the white butcher paper covering the top of the table. We didn't say much. Occasionally, I'd write Keith a note and pass him a crayon to write a response. We shoved the small candle centerpiece aside and held hands across the table. I managed a weak smile and took deep sighs between bites. The searing emotions claimed my stomach space. We didn't box up our leftovers to take home, and we never went back to that restaurant.

## Questions for the Reader:

*Is there something you wanted so badly you prayed for it?*

*How have your "unanswered" prayers turned into opportunities that led you a different way?*

# An Inspired Message

The doorbell rang, circulating inside our newly built home. I wasn't used to the sound. I opened the door and vaguely recognized the woman with frizzy, brown hair. She smiled at me.

"Hey, I don't know if you remember me," she said, a few flyaways blowing in her makeup-less face. "I'm Jenna, from church."

"Oh yeah. That's right. Jenna. Please, come in. How are you?"

"Busy as always. We just finished up another school unit this morning. Michael's spelling just blows me away. He's writing words a third or fourth grader might know. You should hear him talk. It's like a little adult conversation. Ask him about trains. He knows how a steam engine runs differently than a coal or wood-burning one."

I gestured to the couch and sat down opposite her, perched on the edge of a chair. I raised my eyebrows and waited.

"And Cora, oh!" she slapped her knees with both hands. "She's so artistic. She always carries a purse stuffed with crayons and pencils. Her notepad is full of creative fairies and monsters. I'm just, wow—I'm so proud."

"That's great," I mustered. "I was always the type that—"

"I'm sure Seth will be as brilliant as his siblings. You really should consider homeschooling when you . . . you know."

I shrugged. "How has your experience—"

"Michael's so much further along than the kids his age at the elementary school. At first, I didn't know how homeschooling would go, but I see such a huge difference. Now, I can't even imagine a parent wanting to send their child to be brainwashed in a government-controlled public school. I mean, really, there are so many options."

I looked down at my watch and at the front door, frowning.

"In fact," she continued, "when I teach the kids on Sundays, I can tell which parents spend quality time educating them and which ones don't. It's so sad. Since the politicians removed God from schools, I removed my kids too. That's how I look at it. I don't need a politician educating them." Her fingers made air quotes around "educating."

I took a deep breath. I remembered her rowdy, rumpled kids scrambling toward the pulpit the last couple of Sundays, ducking behind the choir director for cover. Their unobtrusive father had adjusted his dark glasses and woven through the choir seats, trying to snag their collars. He'd yanked them sideways, like a carry-on bag, and toted them off to the hallway, barefoot and kicking.

"Well, enough about me." Jenna chuckled. "You're probably wondering why I'm here. I know we don't know each other well, but when I was praying this morning, I thought about when you introduced yourself. I felt inspired to come and share a special message with you about your . . . situation." She crossed her black leather ankle boots, which looked a couple of sizes too small, her cartoonish feet dancing around the word *infertility*. She looked off at the wall, where our wedding picture hung slightly askew over the couch. She nodded and clasped her hands.

"Chani, there is a solution to your problem. It's in the scriptures. It's so obvious. When someone suffered from a disease, the Savior asked them if they had faith to be healed. Those who did—their illnesses were taken away. Some knew they didn't have the faith and asked Jesus Christ to help their unbelief. There were barren women in Bible times. God can open a womb. It just takes sufficient faith."

"Sufficient faith?" I picked the least biting response and chomped on my lower lip to stop the rest from tumbling out.

"He's giving you the opportunity to repent and turn to Him in prayer. Once you are right before God and your faith has grown, God will answer your prayers and heal you. It's been done before. The scriptures are a pattern for our lives."

My eyes bulged, and I could feel the blood thudding in my temples. I parted my lips to offer a rebuttal, but nothing came out. God and I—we were on friendly terms. I spoke with Him often. I studied His words every morning, searching for answers to my struggles. But as the years passed, Keith and I remained childless.

Did this pious sister realize there were still days I refused to wake up? Guilt impeded my total healing process. I felt defective. Keith and I constantly apologized for letting each other down. Growing up in such large families and in a family-centered church, we were misfits. Jenna took my silence as humble contemplation of the revelation she had provided and excused herself, straightening her inside-out jacket.

I managed to thank her for taking the time to come over and share her thoughts but cursed under my breath after she left. It's hard to explain to someone who has a baby annually how helpless infertility can feel. I slammed my fist against the front door, tears stinging my eyes. *How could she? She has no idea! How can someone else question my standing before a very personal God?* She'd assumed I'd neglected my relationship with Him and that my emaciated spirituality demanded God's wrath and punishment.

I closed my eyes and recalled that little blond boy smiling at me in his striped shirt. When the youth at church handed out little purple corsages to the mothers on Mother's Day, I slipped out the back and thought of him. When Keith slept alone in the back seat of our car at the fathers and sons' campout, we held fast to the dream that the little boy still waited for us. God had promised us.

I meet some people who tell me, "I've always wanted to adopt. That's something my wife and I plan to do eventually." For me, that wasn't the case, not immediately anyway. Selfishly, I wanted a child to have my lips and Keith's eyes. Between the two of us, that little one was guaranteed to have a shock of bright-white, platinum hair. I wanted to feel movement, a retaliating kick when I tickled under my rib cage. I wanted Keith to lean down and croon Morrissey tunes in his best British accent while massaging the sides of my belly.

I could paint the portrait of the moment just after the delivery, when I lay exhausted and completely ecstatic, our boy swaddled in a bassinet beside me. I wanted my husband to brush my damp hair from my face and think I was the most radiant woman he had ever seen. He'd fall in love all over again. His respect for me would increase a hundredfold when he saw my beautiful role in the miracle of life.

Sadly, I would never experience that. Not that way. I grieved for that vision. I mourned the loss of the baby that would never grow inside me. Looking back, we should have taken trips, experiencing the taste of exotic foods grilled on wood skewers. I might have learned how to play tennis, serving aces to Keith every Saturday morning in my white visor. We should have invited friends over for taco nights and homemade salsa. We could have spent a few extra minutes in bed, every morning, whispering under the covers. We could have drained a few drops from the bucket list. But we didn't. We focused on finishing school and saving every dime, not knowing the price of our next step.

We knew God would keep His promises, but we had to do what we could to move closer to our dreams. The way I saw it, we had two options: we could adopt or gamble our meager savings on pricey procedures, hoping for a biological child. Infertility treatments and in-vitro procedures boasted a dismal 10 to 20 percent success rate—too low to tempt me. Besides, if we pursued that course, we needed donor sperm and a surrogate mother. *Wasn't that adoption?*

I ignored Jenna's call for miracle-level faith and called the adoption agency recommended by our bishop. I pressed each number slowly, deliberately, stalling for time. I hung up twice. Honestly, I felt defeated. The sharp pain of our infertility diagnosis had morphed into a constant throbbing, a reminder of the family we would never have. I hid my hurt whenever another family member announced a pregnancy.

After a third call to the agency, they mailed me a manila envelope with color-coded pages breaking down each step of the adoption process. I devoured it, anxious to check every box and fill in every line, anything to move forward. Keith needed to digest it. Even though it was our obvious next step, he had to analyze it. I couldn't push him. I set the folder on top of the keyboard on our desk. He quietly shoved it aside, tucking it in a file behind the computer. He needed to process his feelings first. The topic of adoption surfaced occasionally, but the colored pages remained pristine and blank.

We knocked awkwardly on the doors of support meetings for couples like us. Twisting a pen cap in my hand, I listened to tragic tales of infertility, failed procedures, and mounting debt. We empathized with those who would do anything to have a family. We asked family therapists lots of questions. They hugged us, counseling us to rely on and support each other.

Week after week, we began to view the other couples in our meetings as trusted friends, and we revealed our most vulnerable, raw feelings. We all understood. I devoured others' adoption success stories, and hope began to flicker inside me. We'd witnessed miracles. The right child seemed to find the right family at the right time. Keith and I finally opened that intimidating manila envelope and tackled it one page at a time.

I have since learned that sometimes God performs a healing miracle based on faith, and sometimes it takes more faith to not be healed. Sometimes God doesn't remove the stumbling block, no matter how many times we ask or how hard we pray. He wants us to rely on Him, trust Him, turn to Him. God didn't grant me the sudden ability to become pregnant. He needed me to trust Him enough to take a few steps in the dark to find the child that was always meant to be in our forever family.

## Questions for the Reader:

*Do you have the faith to NOT be healed? How can you live with your current challenges and still thrive?*

*How have your challenges humbled you or brought you closer to God?*

# Adoption Day

"Chani, I have a huge favor to ask of you," Alicia drawled as she popped her gum on the other end of the line. I could picture our adoption caseworker sitting cross-legged in her desk chair, her pastel skirt tucked beneath her legs and her flats kicked off into a corner.

"Sure, what's up?"

"Okay, I know this sounds a little strange, but we have a birth mother who needs help."

I frowned, confused but intrigued. "What kind of help? What's going on?"

"She's coming up on her delivery date. For insurance and legal reasons, she has to deliver the baby here in Utah even though she lives in Mississippi."

"Okay. So?"

"So, she needs somewhere to stay. Her parents refuse to pay for a hotel, and no one here at the agency has had the background check to host her at their place. It's sort of a unique situation."

"Is she choosing our family? She wants to place her baby with us?" I bit the end of my pen and closed my eyes.

"Not exactly. She is placing with another family."

"What!" My pen flew out of my mouth and bounced under my chair.

"I know, I know. Look, talk to Keith about it. It doesn't make sense, but she needs someone to help her right now. I understand if you can't, but promise me you'll think it over."

"Alicia, I—"

"I won't be upset either way. Just think about it."

I hung up the phone, completely confused. Keith and I had completed months of paperwork, researching infant birth disorders and praying about race and gender to finally get "approved." We'd stood stranded in scrapbooking aisles deciding between polka dots and fleur de lis for our "All about us" page to turn over to the agency. *Why? For this? A bed-and-breakfast so other couples could enjoy their happily-ever-afters?* I slammed the top drawer so quickly one of the paperclips jumped overboard. I needed to walk.

My sandals slapped against the bottoms of my heels as I stomped through the neighborhood next to my office. I stared at my colorless toenails, frustrated that I still hadn't taken the time to paint them a deep silver. It would only take about ten minutes. I didn't have ten minutes? A gust of wind billowed my skirt, and I grabbed the hem to hold it down. A couple of safety pins holding the seam together brushed against my fingertips. *That hole!* I forgot to sew it the last time I dropped it into the laundry bin.

"Oh, excuse me!" I apologized as I tripped over the foot of a gentleman pulling a brown paper bag out of his car. He stuffed the bag under the arm of his yellow polo shirt and managed to grab a second bag, its broken handles atrophied and limp.

"No problem. You okay?"

"Fine." My autoresponse for when I felt completely demolished.

*We should refuse,* I reasoned. *Obviously, the birth mother is someone else's problem. Our home study approved us to adopt a child. It didn't involve us opening our door to homeless women in a tough spot.* I grappled with not getting involved, fuming and justifying our reasons for walking away. *Alicia will understand.*

The initial anger cooled with each step around the block. My cheeks flushed, and I felt the accusation that I had reacted selfishly and without thinking. Ashamed, I knew I needed direction. I was not in the best mindset to make a rational decision. I slowed my walk and sat on the grassy lawn in front of my building. I bowed my head, trying to block out the cars pulling into the parking lot.

*Heavenly Father, me again. I'm so sorry to keep bothering you, especially when I don't really have a lot of time right now. Alicia just called. It wasn't about a possible placement this time. I don't know why I'm so upset, Father. Probably because I saw her number and got all excited. I was expecting one thing and was told another.*

*I don't know this girl. I don't know anything about her. If she's placing her baby with another family, why doesn't she stay with them? I don't really understand why she needs to be with us. I don't want to do this. I really don't. We've been through so much getting our paperwork in order. It's only a recent thing that we've come to accept our infertility after all these years. Now, it's flaunted in my face? Why do you need me to do this? Why now?*

I hesitated, deciding to take a second lap, panting slightly from the rigorous climb up 7th East. I held on to the bus-stop sign next to a bench where two men debated a *Wall Street Journal* article. Another man secured his newspaper underneath his orthopedic shoe and leaned forward to read it, his hands interlocked, chin balanced on them. His gray mustache shifted when he sniffed.

I let my thoughts wander. What if it was someone we knew? I started running through the list of women close to our hearts. What about Kim? Jennifer? Marie? Linda? Robyn? What if this was one of them? I sighed, knowing I would have hoped for someone to step in and help them in any way possible.

My walk slowed. The slapping against my heels felt less pronounced, less retaliatory. My skirt clung to my sweaty legs, and I headed back to work, thinking of how I would tell Keith and wondering what he'd say.

• — ● — •

Layla picked at her potato salad, scooped out the tiny purple onions, and moved them into a little pile at the side of her paper plate. She tossed her light-brown perm over her shoulder, her curls cascading down her back. I was proud of my parents for inviting us over for Sunday dinner. When we explained our visitor to them, they exchanged a few meaningful looks but didn't criticize. They simply smashed a few extra hamburger patties with seasoned salt and fired up the grill.

Layla's brown eyes fixated on the watermelon rind tipped sideways in front of her. She held a fork in her hand but had no food left to use it on.

"So, tell us a little about yourself," my mom encouraged, sidling closer to her on the picnic bench.

"There's not a lot to tell." Layla chewed on her bottom lip. "I grew up in Mississippi. My daddy's the CEO of a big fast-food company. I can pretty much go through the drive-through and get free food whenever I feel like it."

"Wow!" I whistled. "How would that be?"

"Do they have pebble ice in their soft drinks?" my dad interjected.

"Oh, Dad, don't start with it." I rolled my eyes at him. A discussion on pebble ice versus regular cubes. This was worse than the weather. "Layla, does your dad know you're here?"

"Yes, ma'am, he does. He's not too happy about it, though. If it was up to him, he probably would've scheduled me an abortion months ago. He knew I would've caused a scene at the clinic. He didn't want to draw too much attention to himself." She lowered her voice to a deep baritone. "It's a matter of principle," she huffed. Her brown eyes narrowed for a moment, and she stopped herself from saying more.

"Oh, Layla, I'm so sorry." My mom put her hand on Layla's shoulder. "If there's anything we can do—"

Layla shook her head and folded the flimsy paper plate over the uneaten remains of her salad. My mom offered to toss it for her. She nodded faintly but didn't meet our eyes. I sensed a deeper layer of pain behind the history she'd offered.

She glanced down at her hands and scratched haphazardly at the remaining flecks of polish on her fingernails, then sighed. "Y'all are nice to take me in. I know you're probably wondering why I didn't choose your family."

I shrugged but caught my dad watching Layla, perfectly still in his lawn chair.

She continued. "See, I want this little girl to be with her older brother."

"Brother?" My eyes widened. "Nobody said anything about a sibling."

"Dunno how many people know. My daddy doesn't even know. A couple years ago, I got pregnant and couldn't face my parents. I went to the agency, and they helped me place my baby with an awesome family and get the care I needed." She reached for a napkin and held it to her nose. "Oh, man, it was hard. I couldn't do it again."

"So where is the brother?" I asked.

"Here in Utah. I wanted to stay with them, but the agency said there was a conflict of interest or a legal something that made it not a good idea."

I hugged Layla and thanked her for trusting us with the details of her life. As the night dwindled, I couldn't help but wonder how it must have felt for the adoptive family to receive a phone call out of the blue offering them another child, a sibling—no scrapbooking or manila envelopes required.

Over the next few days, Layla recognized that her presence might be a punch in the gut for us. She apologized constantly for the inconvenience and made herself as quiet and shadowy as possible. I often discovered her in the guest bedroom, napping on my old daybed. I knew she had wandered downstairs to grab a new glass of ice water whenever I could smell her apple lotion in the kitchen. She ventured to sit near us on the couch to watch *Amazing Race*, rubbing the sides of her belly and wincing occasionally.

The weekend concluded, and on Monday, the day she was to be induced, I drove her to the hospital, where one of the adoption workers met us. The social worker waved to me and helped the brave young woman into a wheelchair. I never saw Layla again. I wonder if she is happily married now, fully independent and munching on pebble ice whenever she wants.

· — ● — ·

"If you got a phone call right now, and you were suddenly parents, what would that baby need?" the instructor, Laurie, asked.

"Diapers," I suggested.

"Crib. Car seat. Clothes. Burp cloths. Blankets."

The responses echoed around the room as she vigorously nodded, untangling her ID badge from her lanyard. I looked at Keith, completely content with wrapping the receiving blanket around a baby doll in a tight swaddle. A baby burrito. The other six men in the room laughed at their clumsiness, nervously eyeing their pregnant wives for validation even though inanimate plastic feet worked their way through the loose folds. We mastered diapering with one hand cinching the squiggly feet in the air and learned the secret to the snaps on pajamas.

The cafeteria staff rolled in a cart full of sandwiches and small bags of chips. Though we had introduced ourselves and wore stickers with our names scrawled in purple ink, I remained aloof, glued to Keith's shoulder. Most were expecting a child within the month, the women waddling around the tables, practicing burping the dolls over their shoulders. We stuck out, for sure, no noticeable baby on the way. But when Alicia had suggested taking an intro-to-parenting class, we'd thought, *Why not? We don't have anything else to do while we wait, so we might as well be productive.*

I skimmed through the pamphlets detailing stork bites, soft spots, jaundice, cradle cap, baby acne, and newborn conditions I had never heard of: How to keep the umbilical cord stump dry until it fell off. How to bathe an infant post-circumcision and keep the open wound from sticking to the diaper. Even the pictures made Keith squeamish. I placed each pamphlet and magazine into the recycled hospital bag. Someday I would read each in detail.

Laurie circled her table at the front of the room and leaned against it. She crossed one shoe over the other. "You know," she confessed, "I'm going to be completely honest with you. I am the mother of six children. Three are biological. Three are adopted. In this class, we have both adoptive and biological parents. You should all know there was never a difference in how I felt about my children, even at first. When they placed my adopted babies into my arms, my heart accepted them immediately, the same way it did when I held my biological children."

Laurie didn't have to single me out. I knew she spoke to me, even if she didn't look at me.

She continued. "When my baby boy looked up into my eyes, it was like I heard him saying, 'Oh, there you are! I've been waiting for you.'"

The ripple of papers and the jittery, excited whispers went quiet. I had heard something like that before, but never from someone who had both biological and adopted children. Her reassurance resonated with me.

"But was the bonding any different for your biological kids versus your adopted ones? I mean, with biological kids, you've got nine months of bonding time. They already know your voice, right?"

"They do to a degree, but the bonding process is still the same, like how a father bonds with his children. He doesn't love them any less because he didn't carry them in his body. Bonding with an adopted child is like that. Now, of course, if they were exposed to substances at all, there could be withdrawal symptoms that might affect immediate bonding, but it is still possible to bond quickly and naturally with an adopted child. I promise there is no difference."

I leaned back in the chair and rested my head on Keith's shoulder. He reached up, touching my cheek. These were answers to questions I didn't even know I had. Maybe he felt the same.

• — • — •

"Hey, where have you guys been? I've been trying to reach you all night!" Alicia said through the phone line.

"Sorry, we were at a family reunion. We just stopped at my parents' house on our way home. They said you left us a message."

"Ugh! You need cell phones! Even homeless people have cell phones." I could hear her nervous excitement on the other end of the line. It made me pace the hallway between the living room and bedrooms.

"Someday, I'm sure we'll get one." I stepped farther away from the dog barking at the kitchen door to be let outside.

"What are you doing tomorrow?" Alicia asked.

"Just working. Maybe running errands. Why?"

The words tumbled out of her mouth faster than I could process them. "Can you guys meet me at St. Mark's Hospital tomorrow at 9:00 a.m.? There's a little boy waiting for you there. The birth mom already signed the papers terminating her rights. She's gone. He just needs a family. It's up to you to say yes or no."

"You're kidding." I stopped moving. My hand flew to my mouth. "Tell me you're kidding." I held my breath.

She laughed, a little winded herself. "I'm more serious than I have ever been. You have a son! You're parents!"

"I'm . . . I don't . . . Hang on. I have to tell Keith."

Dazed, I felt my way down the hallway. Keith and my mom stood in the kitchen, suddenly quiet, eyes unblinking, pleading for more news.

"It's Alicia." I grinned stupidly. They suspected that already, I could tell. "She says there's a little boy waiting for us at the hospital. We get to pick him up tomorrow morning!"

My mom clapped and flew over to hug me. My dad rushed out of the bathroom, still buttoning the top of his jeans, leaving his newspaper askew on the tile floor.

Mom leaned her good ear toward us, trying to catch any other tidbits about our baby boy. Keith held me from behind, his forehead against my back, his hands on my shoulders as I continued. I don't know if he hid misty eyes from the room or bowed a thankful head. My dad straddled the corner of a kitchen chair, watching the drama unfold as he retied the laces of his tennis shoes.

I tried to listen as Alicia detailed the baby's health history and birth statistics, but I just kept thinking, *The papers are signed. She can't change her mind. The papers are signed. She can't change her mind.* My heart swelled with gratitude. I never told anyone, but that was my biggest fear. What if she changed her mind? We'd heard horror stories of friends who'd shown up at the hospital, empty car seat in hand, and left the same way.

I sat down, my legs unsteady underneath me, lips pursed, cheeks glistening. The reality and fear of becoming an instant parent slapped me in the face. I concentrated hard on asking logical questions. I leaned into the phone and ran my hand through my hair, trying to sort through all the thoughts in my head. Five years! Five years of wanting and waiting. Five years since dreaming about our little boy. I juggled my competing worries: *I'm not ready to have a family. What if I'm a horrible mom? I start my new job at the University Medical Center in a week. Do I call and back out?*

"What do we do? What do we bring? What do we need?" I stammered into the phone, years of bitter disappointment finally released. *I was going to be a mom. Finally!* I swiped at my eyes and laughed at how idiotic I must seem.

"Honestly, you just need a car seat to be able to take him home from the hospital," Alicia said. "I'll make sure they provide you with a few necessities to get through the afternoon, but after that, you're on your own."

I don't remember hanging up. I set the phone on the table, my family surrounding me. I looked tearfully up at Keith. The name we had stored away so long ago now teetered on the edge of my tongue.

"Tyson is here," I gushed. "He's here."

Keith pulled me to him, whispering in my ear. "I knew he would come."

We didn't have a nursery ready. It was too painful to walk past the open door every day and see a baby's room without a baby. I'd convinced myself that since I didn't know the gender or the age of our child, I couldn't even purchase onesies or socks to stock up. It had helped me cope then, but it left us incredibly lacking now. One phone call and we suddenly had a lot to do.

We all dashed out the door just after 9:00 p.m. in search of an open store, any open store. Walmart's sign shone like a beacon to us ill-prepared first-time parents. Keith borrowed my dad's flip phone, calling every family member we could to let them know we would be parents in less than twelve hours. I explored the baby aisles for the first time in my life. *What do babies need?* There were at least four different brands of diapers. *Which ones work the best? How can I choose between ten different car seats? What is the sucky bulb thing for?* I thought of our class a month ago. What a tender miracle that we had attended it. At the very least, I had an idea of baby basics.

I pretty much swiped everything into the basket with a forearm, no time for user ratings or recommended products. Mom tackled the clothes section, grabbing tiny shirts with "Little Slugger" in red-and-white on the front. My dad tossed in umbrella strollers and a small canvas tent. I removed them as soon as he put them in.

"We don't need these, not yet. These are for toddlers."

"I can buy them for my grandson if I want." He placed them in the cart again.

"The basics, Dad. We just need the basics."

"I know." He tossed in a mirrored toy that played "Twinkle, Twinkle, Little Star." He would have put in a potty-training chair, too, if I hadn't maneuvered the basket away from him. I grabbed green plastic pacifiers and smelled each of the baby lotions and diaper creams as we conquered one side of the aisle, then the other. We could hear Keith shouting into the phone behind us, "You're going to be an aunt!" and "You're going to be a grandpa! Tomorrow!"

We shoved it all into the SUV and slammed the door before it spilled out into the parking lot. Then we dropped my parents off at their house, swapped the bounty from their spotless Mitsubishi to our sedan with its stripe of crusted chocolate ice cream on the ceiling. It was well before midnight when we finally got home, but who was going to sleep?

We yawned and stretched and put on a show of jammies and bedtime, but we lay wide awake in bed, whispering back and forth. We rehashed everyone's reactions over the phone and laughed about my dad's stroller propped up against the wall in the empty room. This was it. It was go time. Would we be good parents?

• — ● — •

Christmas morning eventually comes no matter how many times you look at the alarm clock and punch your pillow back down, waiting for that magic moment. When I was young, I remember distinctly hearing sleigh bells outside my window, but I'd counted to sixty a thousand times before I could finally unlock my bedroom door and check for footprints in the snow. They were there. Santa had come. I couldn't deny the evidence. I had to wait to see it unfold, but it was worth it.

*July 19, 2005.* Alarm clocks sounded all across the valley. To most of the commuters on the freeway, it was just a normal Tuesday morning. I cheated the alarm, sang in the shower, and dressed carefully. This time, my socks matched. We drove around the Oquirrh Mountain ridge and into town, bursting to tell someone our news. First, we stopped at Keith's work, where I waited in the lobby amidst a throng of modern black chairs with angled, metal armrests.

Without a badge, I couldn't access the upstairs conversation taking place, but I could picture it: Adam and Will nodding to Keith as he passed their cubicles. Kelly raised her eyebrows as he walked directly into the boss's office and shut the door. Everyone seeing through the plexiglass walls that something amazing was happening. Keith grinning and gesticulating wildly. Keith pausing for a moment as his face flushed and he swiped at his eyes. Keith laughing as tears trickled down his cheeks, then, laughing again at himself, sobbing openly. I could see the office door opening and his team surrounding him. The boss putting her hands on his shoulders to help him relay his news. Keith only managing a nod as his lips quivered. His friends hearing the news and releasing a high-pitched, united cheer that spilled down the hallway, two flights of stairs, and into the lobby. I didn't really know how it went down. I just got carried away looking at the chairs.

Finally, our magic moment had arrived. Santa's footprints had set a trail in the snow. We parked the car. All we had to do was take a few steps and walk into a hospital to realize the magnitude of the miracle taking place. Keith held my hand, picking it up every once in a while to kiss the back of it. "This is it. Our life will never be the same," he said. We took a picture outside the women's center, our uneaten cinnamon bagels forgotten inside the car's console.

The automatic doors opened, and Alicia snagged my shirt before we could reach the hospital desk. She slung a canvas bag over her shoulder and nodded to my parents in the waiting-room corner, then took giant steps up the stairs, leading us into an empty hospital room.

I sat in the large chair and Keith squeezed next to me, straddling the arm, grinning like fools with hands fidgeting. We faced a regular hospital bed with a white linen sheet stretched over the edges and tucked firmly underneath. Alicia sat down on the bed and laid out a single sheet of paper. Only one. After months of signing documents, fingerprints, background checks, interviews, and invasive home studies that questioned our intimate relationship and every picture hanging on our walls, we were down to one paper. Alicia explained the consent form—we promised to care for Tyson his entire life—and handed us a blue ballpoint pen. We signed.

I clasped my hands to my heart so it wouldn't explode when the nurse wheeled in a handsome little guy with hair slicked back on his slightly yellow but fuzzy forehead. She handed me the bundle, and I stared at him. Keith put his arm around me and watched me caress the outline of my son's face and then his eyes, nose, and lips. I placed his head against mine, breathing in the fresh baby wash in his still-damp hair. For just a moment, his gray eyes opened, blinking in the bright light. It was clear. God had brought us to each other. There was no other explanation.

## Questions for the Reader:

*What miracles have you experienced?*

*Have you ever considered writing down the tiny miracles, God's tender mercies, you experience daily?*

*Just for today, how has God shown His love for you?*

# A Day in the Life

My brother, Nick, had announced that he and his wife were expecting their first child with a fresh bottle of Prego spaghetti sauce. Nick and his wife had stood behind the counter, hands masking their smirks, waiting for someone to figure it out. Keith's brother Clayton had gifted his in-laws T-shirts with "Grandpa" and "Grandma" branded across the front. Keith and I simply started lugging a car seat with a blue blanket tented on top without explanation. Sudden onset infant syndrome. The double takes were priceless!

In the days before social media, word spread through tried-and-true gossip chains. Neighbors peeked out their windows at the growing number of cars parked in our driveway. Family members brought their famous spinach lasagna. Anonymous angels left little blue bags bulging with ruffled tissue paper and receiving blankets at our front door. Our support circle celebrated our new little guy with one of the best baby showers I've ever attended. No silly games. Everyone got a chance to hold the baby.

I never did get around to highlighting paragraphs in the parenting books or writing notes and questions in the margins. I shelved the medical pamphlets from our crash course for later. I'm pretty sure that if I had cracked open those pages, nothing could have prepared me for the feeling of my newborn son lying on my stomach. I stroked his smooth skin, feeling the weight of him on me, relishing his every movement. He grunted and squeaked as his toes propelled him up my chest so that his wobbly head nestled right against my neck.

In the mornings, I rambled to him about growing up on Dewflower Circle and roller-skating in our carport and unfinished basement; about how my dad wandered the neighborhood streets, gathering all the other daddies to toss heavy frisbees back and forth; about my mom painting all the kids' faces for the Fourth of July; about how she sat on the porch and jammed on her acoustic guitar with Grandpa and his mandolin. I wished he would have been here to experience it all—creating sledding hills off the neighbor's deck, burying GI Joes under the neighbor's trampoline, and sprinting to hide behind a dented garbage bin to sneak close enough to "kick the can."

After Keith left for work, I droned on about trekking up the canyon to our cabin every July 24. The cousins would scatter, some to fish in the river, some to paddle the canoe around the pond catching polliwogs. Uncle Mack would draw mustaches and eyebrows on our faces with permanent marker and let us explore the rickety playhouse, overgrown and leaning dangerously to the right. The uncles would stand around dutch ovens, poking the hot charcoal briquettes with one hand and sipping ice-cold sodas with the other. The aunts would label brown-paper lunch sacks with our names in flowery bubble letters. I couldn't wait to sort through the surprises on our way to the Kamas Demolition Derby. If we were lucky, we'd sit close enough on the wooden bleachers that dirt clods flipped into our faces while we munched on our Twizzlers.

Sometimes my stories put him to sleep and I could feel his back moving deeply and evenly. But most of the time, he watched my face as I talked, taking in every bit of nonsense that escaped my mouth. His mouth formed a little O, trapping his lizard-like tongue inside. Sometimes, he smiled gummy, full-faced smiles that closed his eyes each time. I captured only about a dozen of those goofy newborn smiles on my camera.

As much as I adapted to holding an infant without constantly reminding myself to support his head, my heart burst at seeing my husband take him into his arms. He fit so naturally, like a football tucked in the crook of Keith's elbow. I could see him as the dad any kid wanted. Tyson and Keith played peek-a-boo with the dog across the table and barreled together down the playground slides when no one was looking. Keith's confident hands proudly pushed a dainty stroller around the outfield fences of the baseball park, stopping to watch Little League games. He packed a plastic baseball bat in the stroller well before Tyson could lift it.

Keith always cleared his schedule to see Tyson walk up to the stage for end-of-the-year awards. He applauded an attendance certificate as loudly as he cheered for the Student of the Year award. He was the dad who wore his son's number at all his ball games. Those strong arms that pulled me close to sway barefoot to "I Only Have Eyes for You" in the kitchen had reserved a permanent spot for our son by his side. The tenderness of their bond choked my throat, and my eyes overflowed with love for the man I married.

• — ● — •

When I signed my name to that final document in the hospital room, I didn't magically overcome my squeamishness. This new world of sights, smells, and textures taxed my gag reflex daily. Our little Tyson spit up more than any infant I had ever met. At first, I hung burp rags over my shoulders as I rubbed his back and gently thumped out the air bubbles. Then I progressed to draping a blanket across the couch. By one month, I had to place lines of towels across the room to catch the projectile vomit. Welcome to parenthood.

On one particularly rough day, I couldn't stop the flow of vomit. I lost it every time Tyson did. Every time. I reached for the phone and dialed the pediatrician, demanding to speak with the nurse. Tyson wailed into the receiver as I explained that I'd just fed him and he couldn't keep it down. I refused to listen to "Infants spit up. That's normal." I propped him in the car seat and gathered the diaper bag before the call ended. "I'm on my way," I warned.

The doctor clucked his tongue and shook his head when he took my son into his arms and palpated his stomach. The morning sun shone through the blinds, creating shadow stripes across his furrowed face. "If you could guess, how much formula would you say he's retained?"

"I have no idea. He screams like he hasn't eaten at all even though I just fed him."

"And how long has he been doing this?"

"Pretty much since we brought him home. It's just gotten worse every day."

"I'll be direct. I'm worried he's dehydrated. I'd feel better if Tyson was evaluated at Primary Children's Hospital. It needs to happen immediately. Would you prefer to drive, or do you want me to call an ambulance?"

"I'll drive. I know right where it is."

"I'll call them and let them know you're on your way."

• — ● — •

I drummed my fingers on the steering wheel, oblivious of my speed as I rounded the curve on the interstate. I swerved into the circular drive in front of the hospital, unbuckling before the car lurched to a stop. Two pairs of scrubs whisked away the baby carrier as I sat in the driver's seat, my hands on the wheel, the car going nowhere. I eventually found the parking garage and parked unsteadily, crossing over into the next stall. I closed my eyes and whispered a prayer until I couldn't think of anything more to say.

I walked inside and picked up an entertainment magazine missing half its cover but set it down after a few minutes. My foot bounced as I watched CNN's headlines scroll across the bottom of the screen, nothing registering. I looked over at the door, still shut, the same as it was two minutes ago. I wandered around the waiting room, pretending to look out the window. I chewed at my nails, pointless since they were already trimmed short. Tyson had been in my life for less than thirty days and already I couldn't imagine life without him. I chewed harder and faster.

Pyloric stenosis, the doctor told me, stemmed from a muscle at the bottom of Tyson's stomach that had swelled so large it was not letting any food through his system. He drew a small diagram on the back of the hospital registration paper. His black-ink arrows explained the launching. They would perform emergency surgery to cut away the blockage to help our little guy properly digest food. I braved the diagnosis by biting my bottom lip and then lined up for the phone in the waiting room to call Keith.

He must have left work immediately because in twenty minutes, he had his arm around me in the waiting room. I buried my head into his neck, twisting the edges of his shirt as I tried to find solace in a quick prayer.

*Heavenly Father, they just took Tyson back into surgery. I'm so scared, Father. That's my baby they are operating on. He's so little. I know they do stuff like this all the time, but I'm not sure what to do. I pray that you will watch over him. Please guide the doctors to be able to find the problem. Please be with him while I can't—*

I couldn't finish. I didn't have the words.

• — ● — •

A curtain sliced the room in half. The nurse led us to the bed nearest the door. Our little boy slept peacefully in a teeny, blue-spotted hospital gown knotted at the bottom. I lay down on the bed and held him against my chest, careful to avoid the thick gauze around his belly button.

"Good job, Mom." The nurse touched my elbow on the way out. "You dodged a bullet. If you'd waited another day, he could have been a very sick little guy."

*Good job, Mom.* I breathed in those words over and over. Still, my guilty-parent heart ached, wondering if I should have insisted on bringing him in sooner.

Tense consultations filled the other side of the curtain around Tyson's roommate: doctors, nurses, caseworkers, investigators, police, and Child Protective Services. We snuck curious peeks at the stoic toddler in a gauzy turban. The nurses took turns wheeling him out into the hall, circling the ICU. They read him Dr. Seuss books but got only subtle responses. A team pored over our neighbor's brain scan, comparing it to a normal toddler brain. They showed each other what couldn't be denied: shaken baby syndrome.

I always found the contrast striking. The staff even mentioned it as they changed Tyson's dressings. On one side of the hospital room, a storm gathered, circling a little boy in a turban, threatening to strike with enough force to take down an entire family. On the other side, we had been gifted a miracle child after waiting and praying for years. That miracle doubled when, in God's mercy, he had been saved from serious illness by my gut reaction to take him to the doctor. We clutched him tightly to our chests as we rocked him to sleep. But I mourned for the little boy on the other side. There was room in my chair. I would have taken him into my arms too.

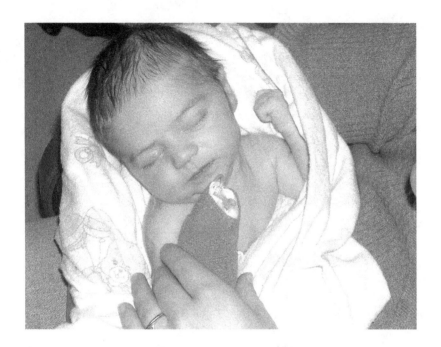

## Questions for the Reader:

*Have you ever felt like you have experienced mother's (or father's) intuition?*

*Has a crisis or traumatic event ever made you feel closer to your family members?*

# Fulfillment

I stood barefoot in front of the sink, stacking plates in the bottom rack of the dishwasher. I raced to load the dishes before Tyson pushed in the rack and tried to stand atop the open door, propelling himself onto the counter. He'd brought me a white plastic baseball with a small hole at the top.

"Mom, pitch me," he said, big blue eyes intent and waiting.

I wiped my hands on the towel and then on the back of my jeans. "Okay. You ready?" I threw the baseball over the kitchen counter, a sinker just inside the strike zone.

He swung, his two-year-old body twisting enough to hit it over the fence. He stumbled, regaining his balance by grabbing the barstool, then chased the ball under the dining-room chairs and brought it back to me. "Mom, pitch me."

"Strike one," I warned as I stacked another plate in the dishwasher. "Two more strikes and you're out."

He swung again, the ball thumping against the wall.

"I've almost got you, Snoog." I wasn't sure how his nickname had evolved, but it somehow fit his personality perfectly.

Tyson wiggled his backside, thumping the cheap bat against the floor to insist on my full attention.

"Last one. Ready? Oh, strike three! You're outta here!"

He grinned sheepishly, the sunlight catching him from behind, accenting his blonde curls and blue-and-white-striped T-shirt. Stunned, I sucked in a breath and sank to the ground. That shirt. That chubby face. That smile. The very same image I pulled from the files of my memory anytime I ever wondered whether I would be a mom.

"Mom, pitch me."

I took the ball in my hands, fingering the rough seam and hole at the top. It scuffed up against my damp palm. I lowered my head, the sun rising confidently in the morning sky. Rainbows shimmered as I looked at my son through wet eyelashes. I smiled and threw the ball.

"Nice hit, Snoog." My voice wavered as I silently thanked God for the snapshot, fulfilling a promise seven years in the making.

But that was only the beginning of what He had in store for us.

## Questions for the Reader:

*Have you written down your feelings about the special moments in your life?*

*Does anything keep you from doing so?*

# The Dream

*You're ridiculous, Chani, you know that?* I scolded myself as I strategically padded down the hall, stepping carefully over the creaky floorboard in front of Tyson's room. If he woke at this hour, the next day would be torture. I tried to steer my mind away from the little girl in my dream. But I couldn't. Those blue eyes, those strikingly light eyes rimmed with lush black lashes, demanded my immediate attention. She seemed so real I expected to walk down the hallway at 3:00 a.m. and find her standing at the top of the stairs. But she wasn't there. Of course she wasn't.

I wrapped myself in a blanket and propped myself up on the lumpy green sofa so I could gaze out the window into the dark, waiting for the sunrise to catch up to my thoughts. I didn't feel bothered. I wasn't spooked. I felt peace—a quiet assurance that another miracle had dawned.

At the first sign of the sun glinting over the mountain, I tossed the blanket over the back of the couch and fished my Nikes out of the bin by the stairs. I closed the door with a quiet click and jogged down the road. My heels pounded to the rhythm of the playlist in my ears as I ignored the pressure building in my right knee. As the sun blasted my eyes, the cogs in my mind blotted out each crack in the pavement and the sprinklers tagging my shins. I focused on aligning my arms, running in a straight motion the way my track coach had drilled over a decade before. How was I going to tell Keith about her?

I pushed my body to sprint the straightaways of each neighborhood, pausing only to catch my breath as I rounded the street names I could never pronounce. No matter how fast my legs churned, I couldn't outrun the question plaguing me: Why was it so hard to tell him this time around? I swiped at the corners of my mouth with my shirt and licked my lips. I could use a swallow of water, but I hadn't brought any. In fact, I had been so involved in revisiting last night's dream I'd forgotten my sunglasses too. I glanced down to make sure my sneakers matched.

I slowed to a walk and stretched at the park, finally honest with myself. With Tyson's dream, I had shaken Keith awake immediately. When the little dark-haired girl appeared, I'd hesitated, fully knowing each step required in the tedious adoption process. I knew it wasn't fair to her. She insistently visited my dreams again and again. But I couldn't easily forget the memory of each of the gut-wrenching phone calls from our caseworker.

I nodded as I made up my mind. That night, after work, I would discuss my dreams with Keith. He would understand. He always did. He might tease me for sounding like the craziest, most irrational person on the planet, but for sure, he would take me into his arms, hand cradling my head. I'd smell Eternity on his blue, pinstriped lapel, my mind would clear, and we would figure it out together. We had done it before.

• — ● — •

We sat side by side on the couch, our miniature pinscher, Daphnie, wedged under a blanket between us. I turned to look at Keith as I pulled my legs up to my chest and rested my head on my knees. As I contemplated saying something outright, I looked at the ground, pleading for assistance to find the words. Would he think I was out of my mind? Would he think I was a superstitious psychic? When I voiced the words in my mind, they sounded supernatural, unbelievable.

I dreaded the truth in those words. I knew who the girl was, and, yet, not exactly. I knew what the dream meant, a little. But the minute I said the words to Keith, they would become real. I would be committed. I wasn't sure I wanted to travel that path again. I took a deep breath and reached down to stroke Daphnie's back.

Keith rested his heels on the coffee table. He pulled a corner of the blanket around his shoulder and played with the frayed edge, rolling it between his fingers. He waited. I watched him twist the blanket and hated to torture him with silence.

My heart ricocheted against my insides. "I don't even know how to start, Bug," I confessed.

He shrugged and cleared his throat. "Just talk to me."

I inhaled enough air to inflate my cheeks, then let it all out through pursed lips. I closed my eyes, taking one more solid breath. "Okay, you know how I had something to talk to you about? I'm not quite sure how to say it, so I'm just going to blurt it out." I paused and shifted my knees sidesaddle so I could turn and look at him. I swallowed the lump in my throat that threatened to climb higher and trigger some tears. "I had another dream."

"Another dream?" He met my eyes, searching my face.

"You know, like . . . before."

"Like before Tyson?" He dropped the edge of the blanket and smoothed it with his hand.

"Yeah, except it's a little girl this time. With dark, curly hair and very dark eyelashes, even though her eyes are lighter. That's what I remember most about her, actually."

He froze. His eyes seemed to forget to blink, and he leaned forward. "What was she doing?" he asked, voice tight.

I looked down at my small hands, my thumb tracing the uneven nails of my four other fingers. I could feel the chips from transcribing medical records at the keyboard upstairs in the office.

Time to clip them again. I hated the sound of my nails chattering against the computer.

"That's just it. A face and nothing else. But I've seen her a few times."

The silence drifted like a mist into the room and settled into the recesses of the striped couch cushions. I didn't have to look directly at my husband to know he avoided my gaze, fixing his eyes on the white wall in front of us. I'm not sure what I expected. Not silence, though. I scratched Daphnie's ears, feeling her roll her head to the side, soaking in the attention.

Keith moistened his lips and managed, "You dreamed about a little dark-haired girl?" he whispered. His eyes glazed over, seeing and unseeing at the same time. He rubbed his forehead, then covered his nose and mouth. He stayed that way as I answered with a scratchy, unnatural voice.

"I'm pretty sure she's our daughter. I think she's waiting for us."

I waited for a response but didn't get one.

"She needs us, Keith," I tried again.

He sucked in a small breath and frowned at his hands for a moment. He cleared his throat, this time with more force.

"What color was her dress?" His voice wavered slightly.

"Are you kidding? What was the color of her dress? What does that matter?"

"It matters."

"Okay, blue. A navy-blue dress with a small white bow on the hem. I've also seen her in a white nightgown. Why?"

Keith sat up and straightened his back, moving his hands away from his face. Resolutely, he took my hand from the dog and sandwiched it between his two hands. "I think I dreamed about her a couple of nights ago."

I started, analyzing him with narrowed eyes. *What? Was he serious? Was he just messing with me?*

He squeezed my hand, his thumb rubbing semicircles over my knuckles. "After my dream, I turned over to tell you about her, but you were asleep. A deep sleep. I didn't want to wake you. I guess I just forgot the next morning. I've been meaning to talk to you since, but I . . . I'm sorry."

"What was she doing in your dream?" I snapped, surprised by a rush of frustration.

"I was holding her in my arms. I was introducing her to all my cousins. I was saying, 'She's coming, but she's not here yet' or something like that."

"What does it mean?" I wondered out loud.

"I don't know. I don't know what to make of it."

I pulled my hands away from Keith and unknowingly nibbled at my thumbnail. I caught myself and sat on my anxious hands instead. I wished Keith would say something, but he just sat there.

"But we both saw the same little girl. Keith, this is just . . . I don't know. I don't even know what to say. I'm so . . . confused."

More silence.

I leaned forward. "Are you upset, babe? Help me understand."

Keith looked at me, finally focusing. "No, I'm not mad. Not at all. Sorry, you just caught me thinking."

He pushed the bundled doggy off the couch and pulled me close to him. He shifted his body, his arm creating a safe, warm space for me. I leaned into him, needing the comfort of my head next to his, both of us overwhelmed, both unsure. We held each other in the lamplight until we fell asleep.

• — ● — •

I still had a hard time wrapping my head around it all. I kept waiting for Rod Serling to come out, take a drag on his cigarette, and pronounce that we had now entered the Twilight Zone. It wasn't normal. I put one foot in front of the other, pushing the plastic stroller handles with the palms of my hands but barely moving forward along the sidewalk. Keith reached down and tightened the stroller buckle underneath Tyson's wiggly legs. I knew he was old enough to walk, but considering the length of the trail and the seriousness of our talk, a stroller served us better.

I squinted at Keith, my hand shading my eyes as we neared the soccer fields. "I don't know, Buggy. I just don't know if I'm ready to do this again."

By then, he was accustomed to our nicknames for each other. "I know. I've been wondering that too."

"When I think about starting over, you know, all the paper-work and interviews, my breath catches in my throat, and it feels like I can't get enough air. I'm panicky."

"Can't they just use our same information from before? Do our background checks still count?" Keith asked.

"I don't think it works that way. I think if we adopt again, we start at square one."

"But it hasn't been that long." He kicked at a rock on the sidewalk.

"That's just it. We're still recouping from Tyson's fees. Where's the money gonna come from?"

"We've got time. Most of the money isn't due up front."

"Are you saying you want to move forward with this?" I stopped, turning to face him fully. Not knowing what to do with my hands, I crossed them in front of my body.

"I'm saying that we can't ignore the facts." He rubbed at the stubble on his chin whenever he thought through an issue. The practical, let's-fix-this side of him never failed me. "You can't deny that we both dreamed about the exact same little girl. That's not an everyday thing."

"No, I know." I sighed, looking out over the grass in the fields bordering our house. Pretty soon the builders would claim that land too. I had already seen a dozen newly framed homes on our walk through the neighborhood.

He continued. "Maybe I would count it as a coincidence except we both felt that she was ours. That feeling didn't leave after we woke up. I introduced her to my family in the dream."

"Do you feel like it's an urgent thing? What if we wait a little while? What if we wait until Tyson is a little older?"

"But what if she's not supposed to come then? What if we miss out because we were scared? Halfway committed?"

"It's not just that I'm scared. I'm practical. We can't afford it. You're still in school. We're barely squeaking by each month as it is." I closed my eyes, slowly shaking my head. I hated to admit it. "I don't know if I have another adoption in me. Not right now." My confession made me feel small. "Why would God ask so much of us?"

We both gnawed on the question as the stroller rolled over each crack in the sidewalk. Tyson fell asleep, head cockeyed against the side of the stroller, mouth wide open. He never slept any other way.

Keith swallowed. "She looked nothing like us."

I agreed.

"Because of that, we are looking at two different scenarios. The way I see it, she's got to come into our family through adoption or foster care. One of the two."

"The timing doesn't make sense," I rationalized.

"But Chani, if it's God's will for us to have a bigger family, He'll provide a way for us, even if it doesn't make sense right now."

I knew he was right. He was always right. Such an infuriating quality. I leaned forward, propping my weight against the stroller as it rolled on. Keith walked beside me, matching my stride. He offered to take a turn pushing. "I just want to do what is right for our family," I mused.

"I know."

"And taking care of my family includes the practical side of things. Can we afford it? Can I handle it? Are we both ready for another roller coaster?"

I smelled someone grilling burgers on a back patio somewhere, and my stomach rumbled. I wanted to ignore all of it. I wanted to walk away. But I had been given a second chance at life. A do-over. My miracle son had found his way into my arms. I knew I owed it to God to do what He needed me to do. And so I kept walking.

## Questions for the Reader:

*Have you ever experienced a powerful, meaningful dream?*

*Or have you ever felt inspired to do something specific?*

# Hannah

Keith absorbed the brunt of the heavy door as I ducked underneath his arm and stepped into the warmth. I sat down immediately on an open bench. I couldn't remember the last time I'd worn my black heels, and I was already murmuring under my breath as I rubbed my ankle. The tantalizing sizzle of grilled fajitas wafted into the waiting area. We scoured the faces already seated, looking for one in particular.

Lisa waved first and elbowed Joel. We probably hadn't been to dinner together since the group date the night we got engaged. The young woman next to Lisa lowered her head, her dark hair falling slightly forward. She buried her eyes in the center fold of the menu. We nodded to the hostess and wove our way through the booths to join the seated group.

After a couple of excited hugs in the confined space between tables, Lisa asked, "Have you ever met my sister, Hannah?"

"No, I don't think so. Hi." Keith reached out and shook her hand.

I followed his lead, only to find a weak, dead-fish handshake returned. "Nice to meet you," I said.

Hannah nodded and retreated to the corner of the booth. The tips of her spindly fingers sorted the sugar packets according to color. A wire tray balanced an assortment of salsas and hot sauces. She turned each bottle forward and twisted off the top, sniffing it. While Joel talked about his latest business scheme, Hannah used the paper ring holding her utensils to scoop up the spilled specks of salt into a little pile.

I shook off my coat and straightened my blouse. A quiet, bearded waiter approached our table and took each of our orders. I strained to read the tattoo scrawled on his wrist. Unable to decode it, I peeked over at Keith. He smirked and reached for my hand under the table. Joel toyed with his napkin for a moment and then looked straight at us.

"So, I guess you're wondering why we asked you here tonight." I shrugged, and Keith remained still.

"Lisa and I have been talking about you and your family. Tyson's such a good kid. We think it's awesome that you've thought about adopting again."

I stopped unwrapping my silverware and set it back on the table. I looked at Keith and raised my eyebrows. I didn't know anyone else knew about our intent to adopt again.

Keith shrugged, an almost imperceptible movement of the shoulders. I forced myself to focus on what Joel was saying.

"So, that's why Hannah is here." He nodded toward the girl, his sunburned cheeks beaming. "We told her about you. And she wants . . . she wants you to adopt her baby." The last part tumbled out of his mouth faster than he could properly enunciate the words.

My gaze went to the small figure cowering on the bench. I wasn't sure if I'd heard him correctly. Disconcerted, I tried to make sense of what was happening. Keith's expression hardened, and he turned toward me. *Adopt her baby?* Lisa put her arms around her sister and rubbed little circles on her back. Hannah's head sank lower, her dark hair falling across the front of her face now, shielding her from judgment and questioning.

Joel cooed, "Hannah, we are so proud of you. You're so brave. You're so selfless. You're our hero."

I shifted in my chair, grateful for the tall, sweaty glass of water resting on a coaster in front of me. I sipped at it, unable to formulate a response. I wondered if her shoulders jerked slightly, hiding silent sobs behind her rigid facade. I looked away. I felt like an intruder witnessing a crucial turning point in someone's life. A moment that shouldn't include me. I fished out the lemon floating on top of my water and plunked it into Keith's glass. He poked it until it suffocated under the layer of ice cubes.

I felt like that lemon. Poked and prodded in directions I didn't want to go and in situations I didn't want to experience. I had seen the movie *Juno* recently and despised it. While it promoted conversations about adoption, the director portrayed the adoptive couple as baby hungry, desperate, and pitiful. *Was that us? Was that me?*

I realized I hadn't responded. I took another sip, trapped without a protocol for such an awkward situation. Did I just say thank you and leave it at that? Did I invite her to the next family birthday party? Did we synchronize watches? Look up an attorney together in the phone book?

Lisa stopped stroking Hannah's hair and released her. Hannah's shoulders straightened, and I wondered if I imagined them shaking. She parted the dark drape in front of her face and looked at us, finally. Her shy eyes met ours, but a fire burned behind them. A strength. Her defiant jaw convinced us this was a determined woman who made her own decisions, not a lost little girl.

Keith answered, but his words tangled in my mind as I tried to envision the next few months. *When Hannah calls, do I ask about the baby first and seem indifferent to her needs? Do I ask about Hannah's health and seem detached from the baby? Do I tag along during checkups?* I took yet another sip, completely out of my comfort zone.

Hannah suddenly got up, claiming she had to meet someone. She gave us each a sideways hug and bashfully promised to stay in touch. We never exchanged phone numbers or addresses. We didn't compare calendars. We watched her trudge out of the restaurant, hands deep in her pockets. Joel and Lisa filled the remainder of the evening gushing over what a good person Hannah was and how hard this was for her. We nodded, and I picked at my chimichanga, boxing up half. I prayed Keith would slip our credit card into the hand of our waiter without waiting for the dessert menu. *No refills, thank you.*

I scrambled for the car as soon as we said our goodbyes. We sat in it, heater running. I placed my palms on the dashboard, allowing the rush of hot air to penetrate my sleeves and stop my chattering teeth, then turned on the radio and cranked the volume, not ready to sift through my embarrassment and confusion.

On the one hand, I felt gratitude for family and friends who were continuously mindful of us. We were pioneers facing a hazardous frontier as we navigated infertility and adoption. On the other hand, this was the most awkward moment I had experienced in my life! Poor Hannah. How did she really feel? She'd hardly responded. What was she going through? Would she have to miss part of her senior year? I wasn't even sure she was still in school. Should I look forward to her phone call? Should I text her to check in? Nothing was clear.

I shed my heels in the doorway and tiptoed into our dark and quiet house. I hit the light switch with my elbow, illuminating only one small corner of our tiny living room. Keith held our sleeping boy in his arms, Tyson's limp limbs sprawled between layers of blankie and jammies. I followed Keith into Tyson's room and set the diaper bag against a wall. We kissed Tyson good night and laid him down, heading single file into our bedroom. We had some talking to do.

• — ● — •

I woke the following morning to a light rain tapping against my window. I could hear muffled giggles on the other side of the wall and realized that Keith must have gotten up with Tyson, letting me snag a few extra minutes of sleep. I rubbed my eyes, feeling the leftover crust of mascara I had forgotten to wash off the night before. I knew I should get up and take a turn with Tyson, but I was exhausted. Everything seemed surreal. I had only to look into the wicker laundry basket to see yesterday's outfit as tangible evidence that the meeting had truly taken place.

I wandered into Tyson's bedroom, smiling at the folded socks scattered all around the room—one of his favorite games. Keith reset the empty laundry basket, and they tossed the sock balls in one by one. When Tyson missed and hit Keith in the face, he belly laughed, his round tummy tight against his too-small jammies. He picked up another sock ball, this time tossing it at Mom.

"Oh, you're going down!" I cried, taking him by that big round tummy and wrestling him to the ground. He giggled as I pinned his legs, with dad pouring sock ball after sock ball on top of him. He wriggled his hands free, determined to win the sockball war, but I rolled on top of him, careful not to squish him. I loved hearing his tough little wrestler grunt as he tried to pull me down too. We rolled over and over, throwing socks and taking turns pinning each other.

Keith settled into the rocking chair next to the window. I hid behind it, tossing the few remaining sock grenades. When Tyson's attention strayed to the box of train tracks in the closet, I ventured out of hiding and sat on Keith's lap. I could picture it: a few Easter dresses hanging in the closet, a pile of headbands with floppy bows in a basket, a dark-haired baby resting in her swing, a pink, fuzzy blanket swaddled around her. I put my arms around Keith's neck.

"We've got this, love," he whispered in my ear.

• — ● — •

The small square on the calendar buzzed like a neon sign, electric energy churning in my head every time I looked at it. I had never been to an ultrasound before. I had seen plenty on TV shows—the dramatic moment where a man and woman teared up at the sight of life swimming just under the surface, gasping at the gender reveal, followed by an awkward hug to avoid smearing the belly jelly all over each other. I knew it almost by heart, and yet I wasn't quite sure how I fit into the pretty picture. *Will I shy away in a corner, hoping they tilt the screen in my direction once or twice?*

*Will we observe everything secondhand from a nurse in purple scrubs scurrying out to the waiting area? Will there be joy at the sight of a little one or tears of love, regret, and pain?* And the biggest, more fearful question of all, *Will she change her mind?*

I would never deny anyone the opportunity for a family. I understood, completely, the sheer need, from the core of my body, to be a mom. Why wouldn't someone else want that? When Hannah saw those little legs kicking at the bubble surrounding them, would she fall in love, even though the timing wasn't ideal? How could I be there to witness that?

Keith came home from work, stashing his wallet and keys in the junk drawer. I stood in the kitchen, swirling my spoon in the red sauce, adding more oregano as I went. He came up from behind me, pressing his scruffy cheek against mine as he peeked into the simmering pot.

"Mmm, spaghetti. My favorite." I leaned up into the crook of his neck, an embrace that communicated how messy my hands were at the moment. The timer beeped from across the room.

"Hey, grab the garlic bread out of the oven, will ya?" I asked as I found the hot pads in the drawer.

He complied but cleared his throat. "So . . . Joel called today. He said it might be better for Hannah if we don't come to the appointment."

I could understand that. I had no idea what to anticipate at the appointment, and maybe Hannah felt the same. Still, I felt a pang of disappointment and tried to reason it away. I shrugged my shoulders. "That's okay. Will they just touch base afterward to let us know how it went?"

"I guess so." He pulled the garlic bread off the tray and sawed the two large halves into smaller pieces. "I didn't ask."

"How is Hannah doing?"

"He didn't say."

I loved the man, but details! I wanted details. I sighed. "All right, then. It is what it is. We'll just wait to hear back."

It bothered me, but I conceded all logistics to Hannah. She was willing to sacrifice so much for us. I could honor her wishes without questioning too much. I tried to put myself in her shoes. She had her reasons. I hoped she felt that we accepted and loved her no matter what. I grabbed the mixed greens from the fridge and lined the bounty on the table. Where was the parmesan cheese? I was sure we still had some.

• — ● — •

I dragged my lawn chair out to the backyard under a gray but nonthreatening sky. The air was still, and I could hear the cows off in the distance—a low, comforting bellowing that made me chuckle. We lived so close to the city, but a pasture flanked our backyard—something I never thought would happen. Growing up, I had been to my cousin's house plenty of times and ridden their horses. They kept pigs for 4-H clubs and raised them to sell at the county fair. I never realized how soothing the sounds were until I had a home right in the center of it.

I loved a good, cloudy sky. Even if it didn't bring rain, it could still summon the celestial power to dampen the lawns, making everything fresh and new. I leaned toward the sliding glass door, listening for the sound of a plastic bowl banging against the table, a sure sign that lunch was complete.

I resigned myself to stand and walk inside and survey the damage Tyson had inflicted on the table. I had tried not to think about the appointment that day, but as I scooped the macaroni leftovers into the disposal, I glanced at the clock on the oven. 12:34. 1-2-

3-4. I always caught that time. Every day. It made no difference that today was one of the biggest days I had anticipated in a long time. Twenty some odd minutes remained until the appointment.

I loaded the bowls into the dishwasher and dried my hands on the holiday towel that hung in our kitchen regardless of the season. I wondered if Hannah had checked into the office already. Maybe she'd picked up *Entertainment Weekly* to see the star sightings for the week and who'd broken up with whom. Maybe she'd flipped through a dated *Family Circle* magazine and then set it down, unable to even look at the spring crafts. She might be sitting quietly in a row by herself, blissfully ignorant of the people around her.

That was just it. I didn't know. I didn't know if Hannah was alone. I didn't know if Lisa or another friend held her hand as she climbed onto the exam table. I didn't know if she showed up at all. 12:52. Maybe she'd forgotten about the appointment altogether.

I laid Tyson down for a nap and began to make my weekly menu and grocery list for the evening shopping trip. *Chicken sandwiches or Swedish meatballs? What do I still have in the pantry? 1:07. She must be back in the room by now. No, if it's a busy OB/Gyn office, she'll still be in the waiting room.*

*Sour cream, cheese, hamburger, bread, milk . . . What am I forgetting? Shampoo, lunch bags, peanut butter.* I focused in, each item taking a place of supreme importance in my mind. I willed myself not to look at the time but gave up after a few minutes. I clipped the half-completed list to the magnet on the refrigerator, then climbed the stairs and pulled out a mystery novel from off my nightstand. Since I needed to divert my thoughts, a little time to myself wouldn't hurt . . .

• — ● — •

I glanced down at my hands, picking at the blue Play Dough underneath my fingernails, then rolled the dough into small balls and stacked them into little blue snowmen in front of Tyson. He smashed them flat with epic superhero punching sounds. I formed a little top hat complete with bent rim that sat sideways on one snowman's head, more like Humphrey Bogart than Frosty. I smiled as I detailed a little pipe, easily caught between the snowman's teeth.

The phone rang. Absentmindedly, I picked it up, not expecting to hear from Keith so early in the day.

"Hey, stranger, what's up? Is everything all right?" I asked.

"Hey, beautiful, it's good to hear your voice. Got a minute?"

"Yeah, I'm good." I sandwiched the phone against my shoulder and rolled some of the smashed victims together.

"So, I just got off the phone with Joel. You know how Hannah's appointment was a couple of weeks ago?"

"Of course, how can I forget? Did she say how it went?" I patted the dough flat and handed Tyson a cookie cutter.

"She did. She apologized for taking so long to get back to us. I guess it was a pretty rough visit," Keith said, his tone softening.

"Why? What happened?" I stopped rolling the dough, stood, and leaned against the counter, my back to the clock that had betrayed me a couple of weeks ago.

"Well, they took Hannah back for the ultrasound and couldn't find a heartbeat."

"They couldn't find a heartbeat?" I whimpered, incredulous.

"No, Hannah lost the baby. She miscarried. I'm sorry, Bug."

I gasped. My hand flew to my mouth. "She what?" I had heard what he said, but the sound echoed against my ears, not willing to penetrate my heart.

*She lost the baby. The baby died. Her baby died. Our baby died.*
I tried to remind myself that another woman suffered. She could have been locked in her bedroom, recovering in only her bathrobe and puffy slippers for days. Perhaps she was relieved. I'd never know. And yet, my own selfish hopes had been dashed with one nasty sucker punch. A miscarriage.

My head pounded, and I sat on the floor, steadying myself against the table, asking answer-less questions to try to understand where to go from here. I didn't care if Tyson flung the Play Dough across the room and left an oil slick on the wall above the thermostat. I didn't care if our new puppy, Brinley, tried to eat it. In time, I would be grateful for how it had played out. But at that moment, I didn't think about the blessing it was to *not* be at Hannah's appointment that day and how God had shielded me from the initial blow.

Instead, I placed the phone in its cradle and sunk into blackness. My breathing escalated, catching in my throat. I had trouble calming the throb behind my eyes. Thank goodness my hair covered my face as I rolled onto the floor.

It would be different if I could sob loud, slobbery, messy cries. But I couldn't. I found myself under the table, staring at the wall. Silent and still. The tears fell, but against an unmoving body. Someone who had just died a little too.

## | Questions for the Reader:

*Has there ever been a time when God shielded or protected you from something happening?*

*Did you ever think it was just a coincidence?*

# Time to Move On

In the early days of our marriage, I surprised Keith with a "cruise" to Puerto Vallarta, Mexico. We drove to the airport, rounded short-term parking, and pulled out of the parking garage before we racked up any fees.

"Welcome to Mexico!" I teased, winking at Keith. "I hope you enjoyed your flight here." I turned on the Spanish radio station and handed him a pair of sunglasses and a loud tourist shirt to wear throughout our day trip. We sat on the edge of the rec-center pool, pretending we were dipping our feet into the ocean. If we imagined hard enough, we could feel the sand against our fingers as we traced messages to each other on our backs. Our drive-thru tacos, burritos, and salsa packets represented the finest local cuisine. As the sun dimmed, we played our wedding CD, dancing in slow circles in the middle of the boardwalk (our living room). A cruise for under twenty dollars, a day just for us.

I'd always hoped that some weekday, Keith would make a show of dressing and leaving for work, only to sneak back through the sliding door. He'd hide a box of warm doughnuts behind his back, kiss me on the cheek, and announce that he'd requested a day off work, just for me. We needed another "us" day. Just because.

I just knew it would happen. So when I heard the garage door rumble a couple of hours after Keith left, I turned to see Daphnie pounce against the back door. I wiped my wet hands on the towel, leaning forward, peeking through the window. The TV blared *Thomas the Tank Engine*, and the British-accented conversation faded into the background as Keith eased through the door. His eyes avoided mine. I pulled the elastic out of my hair and quickly patted down the messy parts, rewiring my ponytail. I wanted to throw my arms around him, giddy at the prospect of a spontaneous day together, but I paused at the look on his face. "What's wrong? What happened?" I glanced out the window toward the garage. "Is the car all right?"

"The car's fine. It's not what you're thinking." He watched Mr. Conductor on the TV give each of the engines their assignments.

"Are you feeling okay?" I prodded.

"I'm not sick either." Tyson handed him a Percy train to drive across the rug.

"You're acting weird. It's making me nervous."

"I'm sorry. I don't mean to."

I waited for an answer, but it didn't come. "Do you want to talk about it?" I asked.

Keith shook his head. He stood and walked into the kitchen, grabbing a banana off the counter. As he began to peel it, his voice lowered. "As soon as I got to work, Joel called me in. He thanked me for everything I've done and got all choked up. Long story short, he said to go home."

"Well, that's not so bad."

"Except I don't need to come back. Ever."

"What!"

"Yep, pink slip. The company's not doing so well. They're downsizing to just a skeleton crew, and my position's not needed."

"So just about everyone is gone? Just like that?"

"Basically."

I watched as Keith put his head into his hands and rubbed his temples. He took off his glasses, his tired eyes pleading with me. My lip quivered, and my throat tightened. I gasped for breath but covered it with a yawn. *We just bought this house.* I had pictured my son posing for prom pictures in the front room with the little girl next door. All the kids crisscrossed the street, bouncing from one open door to the next. I had three spare bedrooms set up and ready to go the minute our adoption caseworker called us to let us know our family was about to grow again. Now, our forever home teetered with uncertainty.

Keith cleared his throat. "I've been thinking about the money on the drive home. Since we paid off the cars, I think we're fine for a month or two, but we really need a game plan."

I nodded, tucking the loose locks of hair at the back of my neck back in. Keith gathered me in a crushing hug and then marched Tyson into the bathroom to the plastic potty. I wilted to the floor next to the tall, formal chair. I never sat in it, just leaned against it. *What are we going to do?* I bowed my head, my mood somber and unsteady.

*Father, it's me again. I know we already talked today. I'm so sorry to be such a mess. What a blow! I'm trying to be brave, but, Heavenly Father, I don't know what to do. Keith just came home and said that he was let go from work. We have no income to support our family. None. We just bought the house and turned in our adoption paperwork to Alicia. I'm having a hard time breathing right now. Please help me calm down and focus on the good things.*

I took a deep breath, stood, and grabbed a wad of tissues. I filled a glass from the tap and sipped it at the kitchen sink before I knelt in front of the formal chair.

*I really am thankful for our new home and the friends we have made here. I know it's where we're supposed to be. I'm thankful for the time that Keith had with his job. He learned a lot from the people there, and it allowed me to be at home with Tyson. I'm grateful for the skills he's gained and the connections he made.*

*I know people lose their jobs every day, but I am afraid. We've never experienced this before. Keith says we only have about a month*

*or two before the savings dries up, maybe more if we really stretch. I'm*
*so grateful we used our tax refund to pay off the car this last year. This*
*could have been so much worse. But I'm still worried. I don't even*
*know where we should start looking at jobs. Should I look too? What*
*if we don't find anything right away?*

*I pray for your help. Please guide us in what to do next. I really*
*don't know. Please let me know what direction we should head. I love*
*you, Heavenly Father. Please be mindful of us right now.*

I counted as I sucked in a lungful of air and counted as I
released it. I did it again. My throat was still constricted but not
as bad as before. I counted again, letting the fresh oxygen sharpen
my view of our new situation. I wanted to take that wad of tissue
and cry until I couldn't squeeze out one more tear. But I'd never
seen Keith act so defeated. I needed to be strong. For him.

*Please, Father. Please help us.*

Eventually, a sweet assurance came, along with the words of a
favorite hymn, *How Firm a Foundation*: "Fear not, I am with thee,
oh, be not dismayed; For I am thy God and will still give thee aid.
I'll strengthen thee, help thee and cause thee to stand, upheld by
my righteous omnipotent hand."[1]

I knew the song by heart. It had spoken peace when I hadn't
been able to run after my accident. I'd hummed it on days I'd hob-
bled through the halls of my high school on crutches, my backpack lashed to my body. Back then, it was a promise that my legs
would heal. Now, it was a promise that I was not alone in this.
We were not forgotten. I rose and walked into the bedroom to sit
beside Keith. I rested my head on his shoulder, he wrapped his
hands around mine, and we came up with a game plan.

First was the practical stuff. We viewed Keith's job search as a
new, full-time assignment. He woke up, dressed, and spent most
of the day in our upstairs office, polishing his résumé and apply-

ing for positions. He attended job workshops and reached out to employment centers. We made lists—drastic, detailed steps we needed to take and places we could go. His network of friends and family rallied around him with referrals and potential openings. Staying busy made us feel productive. It also animated a new thought in our heads: *What if?*

What if losing the job had nudged Keith closer toward pursuing a graduate degree? What if the strange timing was exactly right? What if we needed to be shaken out of our comfort zone? We didn't put the clues together immediately, but after much prayer and a scattering of nudges, we realized that Keith needed to go back to school. We had befriended a couple in our apartment building during our first year of marriage; he had attended law school while she had worked from home. Nudge. The University of Utah had assigned Keith to a classroom in the law-school building as he'd finished up his undergraduate studies. Nudge. One of Keith's coworkers had given him a current LSAT preparation book he somehow no longer needed. The book waited on our shelf, an open invitation to a completely new phase of life. We just had to crack it open.

One month—only thirty days—remained before our savings dissipated. Just as we hit the one-month mark, Keith gave a visual presentation to the state on how to better market their 529 college savings plan. They offered him a job and an enticing master's program opportunity. Keith accepted the job, but we couldn't ignore the thunderous nudges to consider law school instead of the program. We read brochures. We browsed campuses. Keith took sample LSAT tests hovering over the coffee table, highlighter in hand, anxious to improve his score each week. The scores bobbled, then rose incrementally, but we still had many hurdles to overcome.

*"Fear not, I am with thee. Oh, be not dismayed. For I am thy God and will still give thee aid . . ."*

• — ● — •

I lifted the box off the top of the stack and sauntered into the kitchen, squatting carefully to set it down. I brushed my hands on my pants and looked around. Day one and things were coming together nicely. The couches had survived the drive to Provo, Utah, and now parked along the walls of the narrow living room. I had color coded each of the boxes and stacked them according to room color. Thank goodness for the unfinished basement in this condo to store the odds and ends left over from our old garage shelves! It still hurt to not have the extra freezer with us, but we didn't have room.

I opened a box placed precariously on the cramped countertop, the only stretch of food-prep space in the whole kitchen. I peered inside, removing the crumpled brown paper protecting our white, mismatched plates. I began to put them away, quickly realizing I would have to tilt the plates sideways to fit them into the cupboards. I grumbled and wrinkled my nose, then broke down the dented box and chucked it in the corner. I could certainly unpack the kitchen boxes by the afternoon and see everyone asleep in their assembled beds by nighttime. The rest would come later.

Mechanically, I opened another box, reflecting on the conversation at the orientation dinner the week before.

"What made you choose law school?" the professor had asked, pushing his plate away, his wife rinsing the dishes in the sink behind him.

"My dad is an attorney," an overweight man with thick Drew Carey glasses answered.

Another girl chimed in, placing her fork beside her empty plate. "It's a more stable career to have under my belt. I wish I could focus on just my music, but I'm not there yet." She turned to me, brushing her crimped hair off her starched collar. "I already released a CD," she bragged.

The professor nodded at us, his kind brown eyes encouraging behind his dark-rimmed glasses.

I don't know if Keith wanted to tell the whole story, but it tumbled out anyway. The company downsizing. Selling the house as the market crashed. Bombing the LSAT and taking it again with significantly better results. Selling off our basement furniture through online ads and garage sales. Scraping together enough nickels to qualify as renters. It was obvious we didn't fit the typical graduate-student mold.

I still couldn't believe we were starting a new phase of life. It was surreal to hunt online for the best deals on used textbooks again. We choked down the price of a new laptop required for coursework. We stood in line for student sports passes, wondering why we were pursuing a graduate degree when we were almost twice the age of our peers cheering in the student section. But that was the plan. I unwrapped a ceramic mug with a chip in the handle and lined it up with the others on a small shelf.

Our little table fit nicely under the new light fixture, but the chairs wobbled, and I had to warn everyone not to lean back in them. My kitchen window peeked over the fence into the neighbor's backyard. A rope swing hung from the tree, surrounded by a smattering of plastic playhouses and bikes without chains. This gave me hope that we would fit in somewhere in our new, unfamiliar surroundings, even if we seemed out of place at Brigham Young University.

I grabbed the next box, trying to ignore the musty, old-wood smell that hit me as I pulled open a drawer and piled all the silverware in it. The brass knobs and yellowed countertops dated the kitchen, but the carpet was plush, the paint on the walls fresh. We could make it work. "How are you feeling?" I asked Keith in the evening after his had brothers lugged in the rest of the boxes and polished off the pizza on the counters.

"I'm tired. Sore and tired."

"Me too. Especially my backside. I'm not used to this many stairs. These three levels are going to keep me in shape." I slapped at my hips just to prove it.

"It's weird, isn't it?" Keith mused.

"What?"

"Being here. Starting over."

I shrugged. "It's what we wanted. It made the most sense. We knew God had a hand in all of this."

"But three years?"

"Three years will pass whether we are in school or not. The way opened up for us to be here. There's no doubt that we are where we should be." I knew it with my whole heart. After the shattering news of being let go, one miracle followed another. It was so obvious to me.

"I guess."

"Are you sure you're all right?"

Keith took off his ball cap and ran his hand through his matted hair. "Yeah, I just don't want to set our family back. I know that graduate school will put us in a better place to earn an income, but I don't want us to be poverty-stricken for the next three years. I've been through that with my family, and I don't want it to be us sleeping on the cement floor in grandma's basement."

"You're always worried about that, aren't you?"

"I am. It's sort of a hidden phobia. I think that's what makes me such a miser."

"We won't be like that. We'll take it as it comes. Hopefully, you can get internships in the summer to help pad the income a little. If I need to, I can work too. We have options." I sat behind him and rubbed his aching shoulders.

"We do. You're right. Things will be fine."

• — ● — •

I reviewed the spreadsheet, checking off each bill in order, listing the amount and date. I whistled. It was going to be close again. We'd squeaked by last month because someone at church had passed away and donated their canned food storage to the members of the congregation. I'd waited three weeks to let everyone else claim the best stuff, and when it was apparent no one wanted anything else, I took the rest home.

I stomached canned salmon with a little lemon juice and stacked enough canned soups on the shelf to last us through the month. Thankfully, diapers and wipes no longer claimed a chunk of the budget, and, for some strange reason, the laundry soap hadn't run out yet. That green liquid kept filling each cup. For a long time. Those little mercies added up to more than silly coincidences. God was aware of us. We had enough, even when the numbers on the spreadsheet told a different story. We never went without. That was our miracle.

Keith had wrangled Tyson out the door an hour ago. I had found a decent bike at a thrift store and shined it up for his fifth birthday, and Tyson was eager to try it out, even though the wind blew and it was late in the afternoon. I tidied up the bedrooms and began to chop some vegetables for dinner. Tuna salad sandwiches—the dinner of champions.

The front door flung open, and Tyson ran in.

"Mom, I did it with no wheels!"

"No training wheels," Keith added as he walked into the room. His face was red, cheeks flushed, and he gave me a cold kiss as he stood against the counter, grabbing one of the carrots off the cutting board.

Tyson fumbled with the chin strap of his blue helmet, eyes sparkling and proud. "I did it. I rode around the whole circle and didn't even stop."

"Well, he struggles with curves and ran into the grass a couple of times, but yeah, he's a natural. It only took a few tries before he pretty much had it down." Keith beamed at Tyson.

"I figured he would. He's athletic," I responded.

Tyson plunked his bike against the door to the downstairs and flung his helmet beside it. "What's for dinner? I'm hungry."

I cringed as I squeaked out, "Sandwiches and chips."

"Peanut butter?" he asked. Tyson could eat a PB and J every meal, every day, and never tire of it.

"Nope, tuna salad."

"Gross." He made a face and hopped down from the table.

I looked at Keith apologetically. "Yeah, tuna salad again. Sorry it's not more exciting."

"I'm okay with it. How'd the bills go?"

"Not bad. We're good for another month. I'm not sure what to do about Christmas, though."

"That bad, huh?"

I nodded, eyes down. I knew I could mention it to my family and they would gladly step in. The problem was, I could never ask. My dad always told me, "When I was your age, I worked three jobs through school to make it work." *Make it work. Just do it.* My lifelong mottos had evolved into a stubborn independence. Even in my weakest moments, I felt I needed to brave it alone. Maybe I dreaded being a burden to anyone else, especially my parents, again.

"You know, I've been thinking," Keith continued. "So, remember me telling you about this computer system at school? The database thing? They have that system set up for students to earn points every time we look up a legal case, complaint, or ruling."

I nodded. I remembered vaguely.

"Well, I've never cashed in on any of the points. I bet we could just pick a few small Christmas gifts from the catalog."

Another miracle to add to the stack. God was so good to us. The Christmas tree might dwarf our tiny packages with their dollar-store ribbon curls, but it was something. Tyson wouldn't care. He'd eyeball the snow-rimmed window and plead to play outside on Christmas morning anyway.

• — ● — •

I shivered in my winter coat as I sloshed through the sludge left by the lingering lake-effect snow. Pausing on a wet slab of concrete, I pulled a folded piece of paper from my zipped pocket, then checked the address. I had called to confirm, but no one answered. I brushed a finger over the smudged scrawl, not sure if the phone number was correct in the first place. Although the sun occasionally peeked out from behind the dreary clouds, I didn't feel very sunny. Tyson had complained that his tooth hurt, and when I'd poked inside his mouth, I noticed a swollen gum oozing white. *An abscess. Great.* With no insurance and no rainy-day money, the impending oral surgery clung like a barnacle to my mind. I refolded the paper, straining to recall my conversation with the bishop the day before.

In our church, without paid clergy, the bishop gives every member an assignment, an opportunity to serve. At the time, mine was to visit families in difficult circumstances to see if we could find help and resources to get them back on their feet. This was someone I hadn't met yet. I double-checked the name. Maryanne. I knew she had been released from prison about a week ago, but I didn't know if her family could use food, clothing, or transportation. The city used the motel near our church as a temporary stopping place for people reentering society after treatment programs or jail time. I visited it often.

I knocked on door 16, aware of the man and woman perched near the pool gate, eyeing me. Avoiding their gaze, I looked at the swimming pool crater, cracked and empty for as long as I had been in the city. I knocked again, a little louder.

A woman answered, wet hair still tangled in a towel. She'd paired dirty pajama bottoms with a blue tank top. I wasn't sure if I had interrupted a shower.

"Hi there, I'm Chani. Are you Maryanne?"

"I am." A shy, little brunette no more than three stood behind Maryanne, forehead pressed against her mom's legs.

I waved at the little girl.

"Oh, and that's Cassie," her mom added.

"Bishop Jackson asked me to stop by. He said he talked with you. Did he mention that I was coming?"

"He did. I forgot. Sorry. Come in."

"Thank you."

I chose one of the two seats tucked under the small card table. Maryanne sat on the bed, unashamed but somewhat suspicious. She turned down the volume on the TV.

"How old is she?" I pointed to the little girl now crouched on the floor behind the bed.

"She's four, but she looks smaller."

"Hi, Cassie," I said from across the room. "My name is Chani. What have you guys been up to today?"

Maryanne cut me off. "She don't talk. I'm not sure why. When I got out, I went back to Ron's and told him I was taking her, and he was, like, 'No, you're not.' I took her anyway, but she ain't said a word to me since then. I think something happened to her."

Nothing at the motel shocked me anymore. Over the past year, I had learned not to ask about the details of anyone's incarceration. If they offered it, I gladly listened, but if not, I remained happily oblivious—except when it came to the kids. Their harrowing lives bruised my heart every time.

"Does she like books? I brought a small book about a train."

The little girl widened her eyes and walked over to me. I opened it, lifting the flaps on each of the pages so the girl could see what was in each of the train cars. She rubbed her hands over the pages, feeling the smooth, polished cover and reverently peeking under each of the flaps.

"You can look at it. I'm just going to talk to Mommy for a minute. Then, if you like, we can read it together," I offered.

We discussed Maryanne's meal plan for the week and if there was anything she needed to supplement the dinners. Given that she only had a microwave in the motel room, the meal planning didn't require a lot of creativity. I pulled out a list of the foods at the food storage center and marked off the quantity of each one needed. I signed the bottom and explained the next few steps.

"Since you don't have a car, I can just run there tomorrow to pick up those things. If you're home around three, I can drop them off then."

"Sounds good." Maryanne reached over and flicked the volume on her show back up.

I jumped as the little girl slipped her small hand around mine. She gently tugged me closer to read the board book to her. I gladly complied, asking her questions about the book and its brightly colored pages. Cassie shook her head or nodded vigorously, but not one sound escaped her lips.

I stood to go. "Well, I think I've taken enough of your time. I better be off."

The little girl wrapped her arms around my legs, stopping my progress toward the door.

I handed her the book. "Here, you can keep this."

The little girl seemed grateful but set the book down. She wanted me, not the book.

"Cassie!" Maryanne screeched.

I reached down and gave Cassie a squeeze. "What a sweetheart you are! Thanks for reading with me. Can I come back tomorrow?"

She nodded, walking toward the door. Once outside, she mounted the curb and began to balance her way down the sidewalk on it.

I watched her, fascinated. I had never received so much communication from a set of four-year-old eyes. That little girl was precious, an angel.

Her mom, who'd followed us to the door, rolled her eyes, sighing. She pressed her turban towel against the doorframe. "Honestly, Cassie!" she bellowed. "Sometimes I wonder if I should take you back to Ronny." She slammed the plywood behind her.

Cassie's eyes begged me to stay. I wanted to. If her mom honestly considered taking her back to "Ronny," I would lean down and scoop her up into my arms and take her home in a heartbeat. My little girl. I would let her stretch our blankets across the couches and tie them to the closet door and fill the fort with throw pillows. We'd shelter her from Ronny and love her so fiercely she'd eventually be able to mumble, "I love you so much, Mommy."

Cassie leapt to the base of a rusted, black lamppost, then hid behind it. I forced myself to turn toward the road. I thought I heard her moan, but the whoosh of traffic squishing through stodgy snow muffled whatever noise she might have made. I walked away, the salt grinding underneath my boots. I would have asked the bishop about the family situation, but my hands were tied. The next week, the little girl and her mom vanished the same way the water in the pool had disappeared.

I still prayed over the adoption process that had begun three years ago, but secretly, I hoped it would not go through. Not now. I had no idea how we would pay for anything more than canned dinners, let alone the dental surgeon, anesthesiologist, and all the adoption fees. We renewed our home study every January, and not even one person had sneezed in our direction.

But my time with Cassie brought it all back. I would sell the clothes off my back and the plasma in my blood to fund an adoption to find our little dream girl.

## Questions for the Reader:

*It's easy to get caught up in the turmoil of our lives. In those moments, have you ever reached out to help someone else? What happened?*

*Is there anyone you can serve right now? It doesn't have to be something big.*

# The Coca-Cola Store

I walked inside the translucent doorway, leaving the Transformer character outside to trail someone else. Inside, we were high-fived by an oversized polar bear in a scarf who held a tray with a pile of red T-shirts for sale. Old-fashioned glass Coke bottles lined the shelves, some with bubbling soda inside, others decorations to be placed alongside tin diner signs. Tyson ran for the rotating pillars of bottle openers, searching for his name on the side. I raised my eyebrows at Keith as we watched crowds of visitors toss around a dozen different languages and even more accents.

I could smell a tinge of chocolate from the M&M factory next door as we chugged up the stairs to the dining area. Each table held over twenty samples of syrupy soda from around the world. I wandered aimlessly, bending the rims of the baseball hats, not brave enough to try something that might taste like nail-polish remover. Keith chased Tyson around the bargain bins, replacing every pair of socks the seven-year-old pulled out of place.

My cell phone rang, a short burst of Weezer's *Buddy Holly* rattling against my backside. I pulled it out and answered it, not recognizing the number. "Hello?"

"Hi, my name is Aubrey from LDS Family Services. I'm trying to locate Chantelle Barlow. I have an old address and phone number on file, but I'm not sure which is correct."

"I'm Chantelle. This number's the same, but I guarantee the address is probably different. My husband just graduated, and we moved to Las Vegas two weeks ago."

"Oh, wonderful!" I could hear a sigh on the other end of the line. "I just received a phone call from a woman named Josie. She claims she is the birthmother of your son."

I didn't remember much about Josie other than a brief, uncomfortable meeting a month after we adopted Tyson. For a year, we had mailed her weekly photos and letters, only to be told they'd sat in a pile at the agency, never picked up.

Josie's mom and Tyson's birth grandma, Karen, checked in with us periodically. She respected our distance but called or texted every Christmas and birthday to wish us well. We had developed a warm, open relationship and even met her at a park a couple of times. We trusted her advice to keep a safe distance from Josie and the downward spiral her life had taken. And so, staring at the redbrick wall at the top floor of the Coca Cola store, frozen in place, I couldn't help but be concerned.

"Mrs. Barlow, are you there?"

"Yes, I'm sorry. What were you saying?"

"Josie is expecting again. It was unplanned, and she is not in any position to raise this child. She is trying to locate you immediately. She wants to know if you would be open to adopting Tyson's biological sibling."

I held on to the metal railing overlooking the stairs, steadying myself. *Oh, my gosh! Seven years later?*

Keith walked over to me, dragging Tyson with a bouncy ball he'd scored from a quarter in the gumball machine. He knitted his eyebrows as I mouthed what Aubrey was telling me.

"I know. And no pressure, but she does need an immediate answer. She wants to know if you are possibly open to talking with her." She lowered her voice. "In fact, she told me she has an abortion scheduled for tomorrow morning. She figured she would talk to you first, but if you decide not to adopt, then she will go ahead with her appointment."

"What! No, wait! Tell her yes. I mean, no, tell her not to go through with it. We will gladly adopt Tyson's little brother or sister."

Keith nodded vigorously, though still in the dark on the details.

"May I pass along your cell phone number to her?" Aubrey asked.

"Yes, please."

"I'm sure you'll be hearing from her soon."

"Thank you, Aubrey."

"Good luck."

I hung up the phone, suddenly not sure where I was or what was happening. I sat down on the bench while Tyson weaved over and under it. The replay came out of my mouth in short, half-sentence bursts. Keith soaked up every drop. Nearby, one stranger commented on the angel face of the child in the Cadillac of all strollers. The mother replied that they were actively looking into modeling for Gerber. People passed us, eager to stand in line for their sampler tray, completely ignorant of the fact that a life-altering conversation was taking place right under the brims of their Coca Cola caps. We didn't buy anything. Not one thing. I wish we had, or at least held on to a receipt to let us know we were really there.

• — ● — •

Weezer's driving guitars and catchy punk tones sounded on my phone again. It couldn't be. Aubrey said Josie would contact soon, but within the hour? We had just turned off Las Vegas Boulevard and onto Maryland Parkway, passing UNLV. I hesitated to push the button, suddenly overwhelmed, but I mustered the courage and leaned against the phone.

"Hello?"

"Chantelle!" an overly bright voice said. "They told me I could call you tomorrow, but I couldn't wait."

"Josie, it's good to hear from you. It's been a long time." I tried to match her sugary tone, but I couldn't quite get there.

"So, did they tell you?"

"They told us you are expecting again. How are you doing?"

"I'm actually better than I've ever been. I'm completely clean."

I smiled. "That's great to hear. That must have been a lot of hard work. I'm proud of you."

"I didn't plan it that way. I had to go cold turkey."

"Oh, really?"

"Another arrest. This time I had to complete my full sentence. They've got me under house arrest now, so I have to wear this ankle-bracelet thing, but other than that, I'm okay."

I covered my free ear with my hand. I was having a hard time understanding Josie's breathless chatter.

"Are you part of a rehab program? Are you at home with Karen?"

"Yes, and I'm home. I watch a lot of TV and nap. I'm not working right now, obviously, but I've got a new guy in my life named Ben."

"Ben?"

"You'll like him. He's the daddy. He's a banker. I can see things working out between us."

From what I'd gathered from her mother, Josie had hopped from one dangerous relationship to the next. I knew she lived a life laced with scary addictions and behaviors, but I'd never known the details.

"That sounds promising. Does he know about the baby?" I asked.

"I told him, but I don't think he believes me. He said that if it is his baby, he can't deal with that now. That's why I scheduled the abortion. Randi said I should think about calling you guys."

I drummed up the faint image of Josie's sister, Randi, present in the hospital the day we picked up Tyson. It struck me then how much she looked like my own sister—from her T-shirt and basketball shorts to her long blonde ponytail. I still remembered her sizing us up, a scowl on her face.

"Randi suggested you call us?" I asked, unsure if it was even possible.

"Yeah, and my mom. Are you guys open to adopting another baby? I don't know if it's a boy or a girl yet."

"Of course we are. Do you know your due date?"

"Middle of March sometime."

I could picture her with her long brown hair piled high on her head, her feet on the back of a well-worn sofa.

"How are you feeling with the pregnancy?"

"Good. I can't complain. I haven't been sick at all. Just tired."

"Oh, I'm glad. How is everyone else doing?"

"You know Cal, right? Karen's husband? He is still an investigator. He says he'll retire soon, but he won't do it until Karen gives up the café. That's not going to happen anytime soon."

"Is she still working, like, twelve-hour days?" I asked.

"Longer. And she's thinking about opening for dinner hours now."

"And the dogs?"

"All good. Lying right here by me."

As Josie droned on, it occurred to me she hadn't asked about us at all. *Is Tyson ready to start school? What's new with you guys? The agency mentioned you just moved.*

Suddenly exasperated, I said, "Would you like to talk to Keith?"

"Sure. I'll keep you updated on how things are going. I'll go ahead and cancel for tomorrow, but now that I have your number, I can call whenever."

"Sounds good." Relieved, I passed the phone to Keith. I heard much the same conversation on his end.

We pulled up to Café Rio and climbed out of the car. Keith mouthed his order to me, and we stood in line, drooling over the taco-salad toppings on the other side of the glass. Keith talked until his salad dressing sank into the bottom of his uneaten tortilla. His bright eyes and easy laugh made it seem like he was catching up with a childhood buddy.

Josie had no idea what we'd been through. I stabbed at my lettuce, remembering. The agency had stamped leap year, 2008, as the date on the original adoption approval letter. Almost five years ago. We still mourned the miscarriage, never knowing if Hannah would have had a boy or girl. When we were still in law school, a woman on an adoption website had reached out to us, fraudulently claiming she had picked our family to adopt her baby girl and needed money for doctor's appointments. It felt real. Valid enough to make inquiries. But it wasn't what we thought. And then the office staff at the adoption agency had contacted us with a handful of close calls and followed up with us when the birth moms changed their minds.

I looked over at Tyson as he demolished his quesadilla, breaking it into greasy pieces and making a pile on his plate. For a while, he'd had an invisible friend he included in our conversations. He didn't have a name for her, just called her, "My sister." *My sister wants a treat too. My sister wants to go to the park. My sister is scared.* At first, it creeped me out. I thought about the dark-haired girl often. But then I wondered if maybe, just maybe, he might have seen her too.

With the end of law school and the move, I hadn't thought about the little dark-haired girl in months. That was about to change.

## Question for the Reader:

*How do you maintain hope when God's timing is different than what you expected?*

# Her Name

New Cereal Sunday. Keith had coined the phrase well into our marriage and pouted if I ever forgot to celebrate it. A guy who'd been raised eating rice with milk for breakfast, his goal in life was to try every cereal in existence. We stocked our cupboards with random sugary puffs found only along the top shelves in the extended aisles of superstores. With his tie tucked between the buttons of his freshly pressed white shirt, he would smell the contents of the boxes, then mix them with other cereals to develop strange concoctions.

One Sunday, as Keith and Tyson devoured their Cocoa Puffs mashup, I stood in the closet and selected the green wraparound dress with a thick belt just under my bustline. I felt like a '50s pinup in that dress, sleeves slightly folded and full skirt forming a full circle when I twirled around, like Sandra Dee in *Gidget*, or *Tammy and the Doctor*. I flipped up the ends of my shoulder-length hair as the cherry on top.

Keith opened the car door for me. I bounced in but scuffed my heels against the side of the car and landed sideways on the passenger seat. He smirked as I did so. I knew I wasn't graceful, and I grinned sheepishly. He tucked a fold of my dress underneath my leg so it wouldn't get caught in the door, a green stretch of fabric flapping in the wind as we cruised down the street.

We walked toward the brick church building with its sparkling, white steeple. I shook hands with some friends holding the door. My compulsion for punctuality had not changed since my teenage years, but it had been tempered by my chronically late husband. The choir seats remained empty. Sister Hough coaxed the organ into a low, tuneful sound that faded into the background of the conversations of church members beginning to filter through the doors.

I had packed our church bag with an arsenal of snacks and colored pencils to try to prevent Tyson from tossing paper airplanes into the pews ahead of us. It still didn't stop the high fives when his friends passed him in the aisle or the stickers passed between the kids crouching under the benches before the meeting began.

The rows continued to fill well after the clock struck the hour. Though the congregation quieted when a slightly overweight man in a well-cut gray suit welcomed everyone at the pulpit, I could still hear the muffled roar of a toddler with a dinosaur behind me.

The man checked his notes. "This morning, we will begin our meeting by singing, 'Where Can I Turn for Peace,' hymn number 129, followed by a prayer by Dallin Jones."[2]

I opened the hymnbook, the front cover slightly askew from the loose binding. Tyson dug into my bag, yanking out a coloring book and fistful of colored pencils. I positioned the hymn book against the back of the bench to keep the pencils from rolling through the open space. Sister Hough's bent frame plunked out the introduction on the keys, and I hummed along. I knew the song well, a relief for someone who couldn't read music.

The calm melody wafted across the pews. The children set aside the stickers and popped their heads up to watch the organ. Husbands put their arms around their wives' shoulders. The altos' voices soared in the harmony. "Where Can I Turn for Peace? Where is my Solace when other sources cease to make me whole?" I stopped singing and closed my eyes. The beautiful words spoke of Jesus Christ as the source of peace and understanding for troubled souls. I soaked it in even though the dinosaur continued to growl behind me.

When I opened my mouth to sing again, my voice cracked. I couldn't get past the first line. "Where is my solace?" repeated over and over in my head throughout the lines of the song. The organ closed and the prayer began, but I couldn't stop thinking about it. *I will find my peace when I find Solace. Where is she? Where is my Solace? Where is she?*

Images of dark, curly hair and light eyes with dark lashes distracted me from the sermon at the pulpit. *Where is she? Where is my Solace?* By the end of the meeting, Solace had become real to me. Solace was a person, my daughter, not a comforting salve offered by the Great Redeemer. I dabbed at my eyes. I finally had a name to put with the face.

## Questions for the Reader:

*Is there a song that holds a special place in your heart? Why?*

*How did it become sacred to you?*

# Gender Reveal

The water bubbled up from the ground at the splash pad, spraying sporadically at adjacent angles, sometimes catching a parent unawares. I laughed a few times, turning away from the cement benches warmed by the sun. I pulled my jacket tighter and lifted the zipper up to my neck. I watched as Tyson straddled a water jet, the gushing water gurgling around him and blasting into the air with pent up inertia. He shivered, but I knew it would be impossible to drag him home until absolutely necessary.

Tyson screeched as he bounded from one spout to another, nearly slipping on the smooth cement. He cupped his wrinkly fingers, trying to capture each drop of water, then sprinted onto the playground, where he tossed the remains of his cupped bounty onto the slide. He skidded down, not nearly the waterslide he had anticipated. And then he did it again. If only he could get there before all the water dripped through his fingers.

My phone buzzed in my pocket. I lifted it to one ear and covered the other with my hand, blocking out the noise. "Hello?"

"Hey, Chantelle, it's Josie. How's it goin'?"

"Not bad. We're just hanging out at the park. What's new with you?" I winced as the words rumbled out. I chided myself for asking such a dumb question to a pregnant woman restricted to her home.

"I'm good. I've been really hungry lately, though. Every day, I have someone stop and bring me some cheese quesadillas from Del Taco. I don't even know why I crave the tacos there. I usually don't ever eat there, and I rarely eat cheese. This kid is going to come out dripping queso."

I chuckled, knowing that, coincidentally, Tyson would probably ask for a plate of nachos once we got home from the park. Maybe there was already a sibling bond. "Well, take care of yourself. You deserve to have a quesadilla whenever you want."

"I know I do. But mom won't pick me up one tonight. She's mad at me for some stupid reason, and she says she's too tired after working all day."

"Why is she upset?"

"Because I fell asleep again today."

"But you should rest."

"She says I don't do anything around the house. I'm tired, though. And these dogs! They wake me up all the time, whenever someone comes or goes. How am I expected to get some rest?"

I hesitated, not knowing what to say. "I'm sorry. That sounds frustrating."

"Mm-hm." She rarely lingered on a subject long enough for a response. I could hear the crackle of a package opening and then a crunching. Her chewing garbled her already fast-paced words. "So, I called to let you know that I, uh, went to the doctor today for an ultrasound." *Crunch, crunch.*

"Is everything all right?" I tried not to seem overly concerned or eager.

"It's fine." She slurped something to wash it all down. "Just wanted to let you know we're having a boy! Tyson is getting a little brother!"

I stood still, my voice caught in my throat, a noxious lump of fear forming before I could respond. "Are you sure?"

"Most definitely a boy. No question. He wasn't shy."

"Wow, that's fantastic," I managed. "A boy. I can't believe it."

"You're surprised. I can tell." *Crunch, crunch.*

"Oh, um . . . yes, I am surprised. I didn't know what to expect."

"I knew you would be. Do you need the list of names I've been thinking about?"

"Names?" How could anyone think of names right now? "I hadn't given much thought to names yet," I muttered, still adding up all the unknown factors in my head. *Why would I ever need to think of a boy name? I dreamed about the porcelain face of a little girl. A girl!* I'd avoided clicking on the blue boxes online to see the boy names. Only girl names. I realized I still had the phone in my hand. "Yeah, we'll have to talk about that. How many do you have on your list?"

"A lot. I'll text it to you." I nodded even though she couldn't see me. I fully expected an eyebrow-raising list of unique names spelled in creative ways. She gushed over them. I reminded myself that coordinating a name from Josie's list was the least I could do. Here was a selfless woman who'd made me a mom . . . soon to be twice now.

"I can't wait to see them."

"Did you tell Keith? What did he say?"

"Tell Keith? No, it's just me and Tyson here. Keith's still at work."

"Let me know how it goes." She chomped into the phone again.

"I will. Thanks for the call."

"Yep. See ya."

I placed the phone back in my pocket and tucked my hands into the sleeves of my jacket. By now, the sun was starting to set in the sky. I chased down the blur of orange Hawaiian shorts and held out my hand, mouthing "five minutes" to the toothless wonder. Tyson nodded but scrambled away, unaware of my confusion.

I leaned against a pole where the rules of the playground were displayed for all teenagers to take warning. *A boy? How can the baby be a boy? Does this mean this is not our child? Will Josie eventu-ally change her mind? Will this adoption fail? How can it be a boy?* I curled my fingers into a fist and raised my knuckles to my lips as I thought it through.

I held no grudge against boys. I secretly loved Tyson's grass stains and torn jeans and his climbing to the summit of every-thing in sight. His duct-tape inventions and disassembled gadgets impressed me. I would rather toss a baseball than play with Bar-bie in her dream house any day. Tyson could use a sidekick, and Keith would be thrilled with another rough-and-tumble prankster around the house. But my dream? Those light eyes with the dark lashes seemed less distant now that I knew her name. The vision of Solace had carried us through shattered expectations and painfully lean years.

Darkness consumed the Southern Nevada horizon, and I real-ized five minutes had passed many times over. Keith would be home soon, so I called out for Tyson. I gathered his scattered, fluorescent green socks and the array of tennis shoes, sunglasses, and whiffle balls from around the park. We could never just leave and go to the park, we always had to take half the garage with us.

Tyson hopped on his scooter and glided gracefully down the trail toward the street. I knew I should make him put on his shoes, but he'd sailed down the hill toward our front door before I could even sort out the wet socks. I rounded the corner, my thoughts still entrenched in the gender reveal. A boy?

I squared my shoulders. This baby must not be mine. Some-thing would happen. Something would stop the process. Josie would change her mind and decide to parent this baby. Ben could derail it. The tattered agency might not possess the credentials to handle the logistics by the end of it all. Every roadblock and tragic dead end loomed large.

As I had so many times before, I began to build a wall around my heart. Every brick, every layer of mortar, stone on stone, insulating it against the worst possible scenario. I resolved I would not think about this baby boy at all.

## Questions for the Reader:

*Has there ever been a time in your life when you wondered how things would work out? You just couldn't see how all the pieces would fit together? What happened?*

# At the Hospital

*March 13, 2013*

I could remember 3/13/13, our thirteenth year of marriage. When the call vibrated in my back pocket exactly on the due date, a perky Josie giggled as she pranced out the door to the hospital. I think she expected me to burst into tears or dramatically scream into the receiver. But I didn't. For me, she could have been a recorded voice confirming an appliance delivery between 10:00 a.m. and 2:00 p.m. In fact, I might have been more excited about a new washer. Honestly, the call terrified me. Not because we didn't want this new baby to be part of our family. The exact opposite was true. The initial shock of the gender reveal had softened, and I felt an unexplainable sweetness as I thought of the new baby. A bond. And for the last four months, I had dreaded a last second, soul-crushing, change of mind.

Keith returned from work, and we packed in anguished silence. Nothing was official yet. Josie could hear those stilted little cries for the first time and fall completely for her son. I don't remember if I told Tyson about his new sibling. As far as he knew, we were loading the car for a spontaneous trip to grandma's. As we plodded north on I-15, Karen called shortly after midnight to announce that Josie had delivered a healthy baby boy after a tremendously difficult labor.

• — • — •

It seemed improbable to be standing in front of the hospital, taking the same pictures outside the women's center as we had almost eight years ago. Same birth mom. Same hospital. But this time, I had to force myself to go inside.

We rode the elevator up to the second level and greeted a round, pink woman stationed at the front desk. She escorted us into an empty hospital room and gestured with a manicured hand for us to sit down. Keith sat on the bed, and I took the upright chair in the corner. Tyson wandered the room, touching every cord, every muted button, and opening every drawer and cupboard. He climbed onto the round stool, shoving off with one foot and spinning until he ran into the bed frame or wall.

My shoulders rounded, pulled high up to my ears, knots of tension forming along my shoulder blades. I rubbed the base of my neck, then exhaled, my sweaty palms facedown on my jeans and fumbling with imaginary loose threads. I had learned that if I focused, I could mentally slow down my heart rate. It didn't work this time. The nondescript white clockface on the wall ticked away each second we didn't hear anything. Each damning second before bad news slithered through the door. Keith watched me, and I watched the clock, both of us frowning.

A timid knock preceded an apologetic nurse in blue scrubs. "I know you've been waiting, Mr. and Mrs. Barlow. We are still trying to get all the documents in order for you. I know it's been over an hour."

"Is anything wrong?" I raised my chin, waiting for the downpour.

"Well, you should probably know that the birth father is here. He was here for the delivery last night. Ever since then, he has been hesitant to sign the documents."

"Why? What happened?" I choked out. "The last time I talked to Josie, I thought he was out of the picture a long time ago."

"Apparently, he knew Josie was expecting. She informed him at the beginning that he was the father, but he never believed her."

I twisted my hair around my finger. "How did he end up here for the delivery?"

"She must have called him at some point. He made it in time for the birth. When he saw the little boy . . . when you see him . . . I mean, there's no question he's the father."

I stood and walked over to the hospital bed. "What can we do?" I asked.

"Nothing, other than wait. I will let you know if anything happens."

· — ● — ·

I paced the room, finally remembering to shed my jacket. I plucked at my shirt, trying to dry the wet circles blooming under my arms. I folded my arms over them, then walked to the window, staring at the closed blinds. The empty car seat waited in the corner. There was nothing I could do to provide an occupant. I was powerless. I sat down on the rolling stool, closed my eyes, and leaned my head against the wall, drumming my fingers and bobbing my knee up and down.

Keith took Tyson down the hall to plunder the vending machines. They returned, pockets bulging and Tyson grinning from the leftover quarters he'd tucked into his pants. I pulled the stool over to the counter and showed Tyson how to flick a quarter, spinning it so fast you couldn't see it. He slapped it flat and asked for a turn. We texted our family, "Nothing," and then paced the room again.

Two smiling caseworkers pushed open the door and stepped inside. Both hugged manila folders to their chests. In true Game Show Network fashion, I waited for one to turn her folder around and hold it up to the camera. The other caseworker's answer could possibly match it.

"Okay, so we have good news and bad news. The good news is that Ben signed the papers relinquishing his parental rights."

I held my breath. I wanted to grin. I wanted to be so blissfully relieved that when I crossed the room to hug Keith, I tripped and fell into his arms. But I didn't. I fixed a cynical gaze on her face.

She avoided my eyes and straightened the papers in the folder. "The bad news is that his parents are here at the hospital. They want to talk to you."

I looked at Keith, unease settling into the lines around my tight mouth. "They want to talk to us? Why?"

"I'm not sure. I think they just want to meet you."

"But he signed the papers, right? And Josie? There's nothing these people can do to stop this from happening?"

"Everything is signed and done."

I smoothed my hair flat on my head, closing my eyes and processing the news, then leaned against the wall and exhaled a lungful of pent-up tension. I could feel the weight lift to a slightly more manageable amount.

"Can we see the baby?" Tyson asked.

"Of course you can."

We gathered the candy-bar wrappers and straightened the sheets on the hospital bed we had used as a couch to watch *American Pickers* on TV. Keith grabbed the empty car seat, and we followed the caseworkers down the hall and into another wing of the hospital.

The door was open, and we could hear a talk show roaring on the TV as well as a few voices. As we entered, Josie propped herself up in bed, dark hair piled high in a messy bun. She wore a gray hospital frock, far too bulky for her petite shoulders. She smiled wide enough to reveal the gap between her front teeth and patted a spot on the bed.

"Hey, you're here. I wasn't sure where you guys were."

I pulled a strand of hair off my shoulder. "They had us in another room down the hall. We've just been hanging out."

Karen piped up. "It was Ben. It was all him. I told him that he better sign those papers or else."

The caseworker leaned closer. "You should have heard them going at it. There was yelling and everything."

Karen gloated. "You bet I yelled at him. Damned if he's going to ruin this for my grandson just because he wants to be a big, happy family all of a sudden."

"What happened?" I asked.

"Oh, we was closin' up down at the café when Josie's water broke yesterday. That's when she called you to come. But after she was done talkin' to you, she called Ben, and he come down too." I could picture Karen behind the counter in the back of the restaurant, stirring gravy for the roast-beef special she'd served last night. The orange tiles were clean but clearly old, the dark wood on the booths not necessarily inviting but a perfect dive-y setting for a home-cooked meal.

"I thought Ben was out of the picture months ago."

"We did, too, until she called him up. He stayed the whole night, and I told him if he's gonna stay, he's not gonna stay in the same room as Josie, and I'll make sure of that."

"So he was there for the birth?" I asked.

"Yeah, he was in the room for it all, but he don't really want much to do with it. They offered to let him cut the umbilical cord, but he wouldn't."

"That's probably what Keith would do too." It was funny to try to picture Keith in a medical setting, strong and dedicated to his family but losing his lunch in the corner. He cowered at the sight of blood. Medical terms made him uncomfortable.

"You shoulda heard Josie scream. By the time we was at the hospital, it was too late for an epidural. She had to go completely natural, and every room down this hall knew it. She was screamin' bloody murder, and I was screamin' at Ben to get out, but he just stayed there, refusing to leave."

"Where is Ben now?"

"He left about twenty minutes ago, after he signed the papers."

"But his parents are here?"

Karen's face clouded, and she pursed her lips. "They're here. Don't know where, but they're here."

I looked up at Josie, somehow forgotten in the exchange. "How are you feeling this morning?"

"I'm just exhausted. I caught a little nap this morning when they wheeled him away, but I could use another."

"Do you want us to step out so you can sleep?"

"No, no. Stay here." Josie pulled at the hospital gown, tucking it tighter behind her. "The nurse will bring Pi back in just a minute."

"Pi?"

"Yeah, that's what we're calling him since he was born on Pi Day. You know, 3.14?"

"That's right. He was born after midnight," I remembered.

"Have you decided on a name?"

"We narrowed it down. We also wanted to see if you had any names you felt strongly about."

"Well, Ben did have a suggestion. How do you like Dallas?"

"Dallas? As in the city?"

"As in the Dallas Cowboys."

"You want to name the baby after the Dallas Cowboys?"

"Well, that's Ben's favorite team."

I glanced at Keith, who was biting his bottom lip in the corner, stifling a smirk. I knew there was no way on earth he would name his son after the Dallas Cowboys.

"It's not bad," I said. "We'll think about it. Oh, we brought this for you." I rummaged through my purse to find the black velvet box. "I'm sorry I didn't have time to wrap it."

Josie didn't know it, but we had spent a good chunk of the six-hour drive trying to think of a gift that conveyed our love for her. We had explored every nook of multiple jewelry-stores, lifting golden pendants and rings with precious stones into the light. When I found an eternity medallion knotted at the end of a silver chain, uniting mother and child, we knew it was made for her. We would be forever grateful to the selfless mother who'd made our family possible.

I had a tissue ready in my pocket to offer to her when she opened the box. But Josie barely peeked at it before she snapped the box shut and chucked it onto the chair next to a stack of clothing bags. "Thanks," she mumbled.

I risked a glance at Keith. He shrugged.

The door opened, and a nurse in cheerful Sponge Bob scrubs wheeled in a cart. "Here's the man of the hour," she chirped.

There he was. Tiny and perfect. All bundled up in a white blanket with a turquoise and maroon stripes, hands swaddled against his body, fingers appearing only randomly to flutter against his face. Josie removed the little blue cap covering his head.

"Look at this mess of hair," she said. "Can you believe how dark it is?"

It was almost black. With his eyes shut, hues of blue, yellow, and pink surrounded his eyelids, like he wore makeup. Was it just me, or did his eyes seem almond-shaped? He clucked his tongue and stretched against the blanket. When he couldn't get a hand free, he contorted his little mouth and nose and squawked. A strong leg and arm burst through the cocoon.

"Uh-oh. Someone looks hungry." The nurse dashed out the door and returned with a ready-made bottle of formula, complete with a nipple on top. "Okay, who wants the honor?"

I looked around at the faces in the room but conceded to let Josie call the shots. This was her hospital room, her baby.

"I will." She took him roughly into her arms and crammed the bottle into his mouth. The little guy gulped hungrily. A stream of formula ran down his chin and settled into the groove of his pudgy neck. I resisted the urge to reach down and wipe away the sticky liquid. I would have my turn soon enough. We only had one last hurdle, and it was a big one.

•—●—•

At the far corner of yet another hospital room sat a heavy-set woman with bleached-blonde hair and a pile of tissues soaked with mascara specks and blue eyeshadow.

She managed a half smile while holding a snotty, shredded tissue to her nose. Her husband sat with his arm protectively around the back of her chair. His red-varnished face beamed as he looked at his significantly older wife—a decade at least. He turned to face us and spoke first since the woman couldn't seem to catch her breath.

"It really is nice to meet you," he said. "I'm Trent, Ben's step-father. This is Sheila." He had a nasal, cartoonish-sounding voice that betrayed his excessive height and protruding belly. His goatee seemed so precise it looked painted on.

"Please ignore my crying," Sheila snorted, chin twitching. "We only found out that we had a grandson a couple of hours ago. He's our first. And now we're never going to see him again." She wailed, reaching for another tissue with a trembling, spotted hand.

I shuffled my feet, an attempt at a sympathetic smile pasted on my lips. I felt trapped by the desire to impress these strangers and a knee-jerk reaction to run away. I really tried to put myself in their shoes, to wonder what it would be like to have the very first grandbaby taken and raised by some random family. Her heavy-laden drama made me feel like a horrible person, a baby-snatching Grim Reaper tearing a helpless newborn from the shaking hands of decent people. I couldn't meet their gaze.

Thankfully, Keith rescued me by calmly sitting down at the table, Tyson on his lap. With firm handshakes, he introduced us all, keenly interested in them and their family. Trent answered kindly, but Sheila blubbered inconsolably, "How could Benny do this to me?" "Benny" was a perfect child, apparently, and couldn't be at fault, even in this circumstance. Sheila blamed Josie for everything, for forcing herself on her son and entrapping him.

She begged us for daily baby pictures and progress updates. I couldn't imagine fulfilling such a contract with this irrational woman.

"I know I won't be thought of at the high school graduation, but could you at least send me an invitation? Will you send him to college? No one in our family has graduated college. That would be a tremendous blessing to our family."

Trent awkwardly shushed his spouse and straightened her top, which had slipped down low enough to reveal her bra straps. He looked at us directly.

"You will call us periodically, won't you?" It was less a question and more of a statement.

I glanced at the caseworkers packed into the room, hiding behind their manila envelopes, clearly never trained for such circumstances as this. They shrugged. Oh, how I missed Alicia! She always knew how to lighten the mood during awkward moments.

"I'm sorry, but for now, we're planning on weekly updates online, and we can email you pictures at least for the next year. We're open to talking again at that point," I said, hoping it was enough. I didn't feel like bartering.

The woman heaved a tremendous sigh and blew her nose. "I'm sure that's how it is with these adoptions. You just take the baby and run. You seem like nice enough people, though. I thought we might actually have a chance to see him as he grows up."

Trent straightened to his full height and interrogated Keith. "So, where do you guys live? Do you ever intend to adopt more kids? Have you already looked into the schools? Will you support his hobbies? What do you do for work? Do you make enough to support a family?"

The room spun. My phone rang in my pocket, and I could hear notifications sounding. Our families had waited for hours with no updates as to whether this placement was actually going to happen. I knew they were restless. Keith leaned back in his chair, directly answering each question, emphasizing his words with his expressive hands. I perched on the arm of Keith's chair, one eye on him, the other monitoring our eight-year-old.

Tyson rummaged through all the drawers in the room, finding a remote control and clicking each button in sight until a nurse poked her head in to check on us. I resented the line of questioning assumed by this shiny-faced, self-proclaimed prosecutor. We'd been through enough. Luckily, Tyson provided a good diversion.

I stood and redirected our boy. "I apologize, but we really do need to get home to run off some energy. He's had a long day. I'm sure you can understand."

We swapped phone numbers, tucking the small squares of ripped hospital paper into our pockets. When Sheila left with traces of gray makeup lines down her cheeks, we let out a collective breath. "That was brutal," I complained.

## Questions for the Reader:

*Have you ever reached the end of a huge trial, looked back at it, and found you grew stronger?*

*In what ways did you grow?*

# Oh, the Joy

Finally, in the quiet downstairs bedroom of my parents' house, I laid my sleeping son in the cradle my grandpa had constructed for me as a baby. I pictured a backwoods logger in a dingy tank top sanding wooden bicycle rims with gloved hands, the gloves covering the scar from his amputated sixth finger. With a gruff smirk and a toothpick hanging out of his mouth, he probably gifted the cradle to his daughter, nodding and uttering less than a sentence. His tender actions always expressed more love than he was ever able to convey with words. I'm sure she hugged him around the middle, smelling the black coffee on his shirt. I proudly placed my peaceful little man inside, though his tiny, wrapped bundle didn't take up much of the space at all, then gently rocked it side to side, probably with the same awe my mom experienced when I was little.

My parents crisscrossed the kitchen above my room. I knew every creak in the floorboards and could tell from their steps what they were doing. The slipper steps and a short whistle meant my mom had warmed up some water in the teakettle. My dad's heavy boot treads snuck over to the corner cabinet, most likely to unwrap a chocolate-mint truffle. It was as though I could see them through an infrared camera pointed at the ceiling.

My entire teenage world had existed within these walls. In fact, I could still picture the room the way it was when I was seventeen. A giant floor-to-ceiling clock hung on the diagonal corner wall. My CD player perched next to an alphabetized stack of my favorite CDs on the top wicker shelf. My daybed boasted navy-blue and white stripes. No heart-throb posters marred my color coordination and clean lines. If I looked closely, I could probably find rogue pieces of confetti left over from a date asking me to homecoming in 1997. The paper specks had taken refuge inside the matted tresses of the carpet and refused to come out, no matter how many times I vacuumed.

As I looked around, the nostalgia ebbed, and the room changed. The same gray carpet, the same wallpaper halfway up the walls, but now, a hand-carved cradle with my new son replaced my old daybed. It seemed so out of place and yet so right. I could hear Tyson's deep, even breathing from the pile of fleece blankets on the other side of the room. Keith snuck up behind me, arms encircling my torso and scruffy chin on top of my shoulder. He whispered, "Does it feel real yet?"

"No, not yet." With our first adoption, I'd carted Tyson's generic hospital diaper bag as though I was babysitting for someone else. I'd analyzed the can of formula, smoothing out the white dust to an exact two ounces. For weeks, I'd swaddled him on his back when he slept and scrubbed his forehead to prevent cradle cap. I'd washed his pacifier whenever it fell. I'd played the role. Maybe it had been the sleep deprivation or the Johnson's baby wash permeating my bathroom, but I'd felt like a mom. I don't know when the realization actually came, but it did. I knew it would this time too.

As I relaxed into my husband, I released a sigh I had held for the last fifteen hours. I had fully expected to return home from the hospital with an empty car seat. I'd braced for a hospital social worker in a gray suit with flat, sensible heels to softly tell me that Josie had changed her mind, that the right baby would come at the right moment, and that time would lessen the heartache. Instead, my crumpled purse, which hung from the doorknob, contained airtight legal documents signed by everyone involved. In ink. The desk lamp near the edge of the headboard shelf illuminated my TWO sleeping sons. I turned around and pulled Keith closer, holding him in a grateful hug, tracing his shoulder blades with the tips of my fingers.

No, it didn't feel real. None of it did. How did I ever deserve to be so blessed?

• — ● — •

I clutched the puffy blanket with tiny blue embroidered triangles tightly to my chest. When a few raindrops weaseled down my neck and inside the torn hood of my jacket, I pulled the zipper up to my throat. My sun-bleached hat darkened with each splatter and kept my greasy hair from frizzing and matting in the cold. I swiped at my nose with the damp sleeve of my jacket, then looked down. I wasn't sure how much of the moisture was seeping through and onto little Cade. The team mom wore oversized Hollywood sunglasses, even in the rain, and thundered up the bleachers to rail on me for missing Tyson's opening game of the season. She spouted off about integrity and the importance of honoring commitments but cooed when she saw the small infant hidden inside the blanket (our excuse for missing opening day).

The umpire waddled over to the fence and extracted a plastic water bottle. He glugged a couple of swallows, coughed into the sleeve of his shirt, then yanked the mask over his face as Tyson strutted inside the chalked circle and grinned at the crowd. He wiggled to stay loose and took a few practice swings as he watched the pitcher warm up. Then he positioned the bat behind his shoulders and stretched his arms. I didn't recognize the bat. He never seemed to use the same one. Even the newest BBCore bat he'd insisted on getting hung in the dugout with the rest of the gear, waiting to be chosen.

I pounded the metal bleacher with my one free palm, ignoring the small puddle forming on it. "Let's go, T-BAR!" I chanted. I never knew if he could hear me, but I shouted as if my voice alone recharged his hunger for a hit. I cupped my hand around my mouth and yelled, "Go get 'em, Snoog!" then whistled, forgetting the sleeping bundle. A startled baby bobbled his head and lifted off my chest, frowning, his bottom lip protruding. Eyes now open, the tiny Pterodactyl squeaked out a protest. I patted his back and swayed side to side, relishing his squirming warmth against me.

Tyson dug a foothold in the muddy red dirt and lifted his elbows, his jaw working a wad of Big League Chew. The pitcher placed one low and away. Tyson swung through, and I resisted correcting the placement of his front foot. Then he reset, the top of the bat twitching behind him.

Keith watched from behind the plate, his phone pressed up against the dented fencing. "Way to go, Cubbies!" he screeched. I watched my husband rattle the fence between pitches. Oh, how he loved this, craved this. Tyson pounded a double to right field, easily running the bases and sliding into second in the misty rain.

I grinned. I had seen that slide develop over many trips to Walmart's polished floors. As I gathered milk and bread in the shopping cart, Tyson would sprint up and down the aisles, suddenly dropping his body, feet first, to see how far he could slide. A coach never did teach him the mechanics. They were just there, woven into his DNA.

Keith snapped pictures of the double on his phone, then wiped off the screen. He popped a handful of dill-pickle sunflower seeds into his mouth and crouched next to the cooler at the bottom of the stands. Another baseball dad slapped him on the shoulder, and Keith laughed.

I peeked down at a sleeping Cade, finally settled again after my outburst. We had gratefully named him after one of my heroes, not a football franchise. His dark eyelashes rested against the cotton cover. They often reminded me of another pair of dark lashes and curly, dark hair. I shivered, but not because of the cold. I never doubted Cade's place in our family. We knew he was meant to be our son, but I also knew there was someone else out there, waiting.

Behind the third base line, the coach stood in a wide stance in his basketball shorts. He signaled my baller to steal, pulling on the bill of his cap and tapping his earlobe. Tyson nodded. He took a giant lead off second, twitching with nervous energy, like Jackie Robinson in the movie he had seen over the weekend. The batter swung, twisting himself around, and the catcher bobbled the ball behind him. Tyson streaked to third. Safe! It wasn't even close.

Keith stood next to the dugout, fingers curled through the metal grate. Tyson teased the pitcher, jumping off third base as soon as the hurler's focus turned toward the batter. The pitcher hesitated, his cap shading his eyes, then threw third to catch Tyson off guard, but a dive into the dirt kept the Cubbies alive. Tyson loved this cat and mouse. He hopped off the base, daring the pitcher to do it again.

One of the parents shoved two sausage fingers into his mouth and released a whistle, the shrill tone startling Cade. A slow wail came from the blanket. I bounced him a couple of times, cradling his head against me. "Shhh. It's okay. Shhh." Lifting the blanket, I found a beet-red face gasping for air, readying for the next scream. *Oh, great!* I thought as I picked my way down the bleachers past half-empty popcorn bags and Old Maid card games.

Keith turned and mouthed, "Do you want me to take him?"

I shook my head. I wanted to see Tyson score, but Keith shouldn't miss it either, so I paced the length of the first base-line with my bundle. Thankfully, the rain stopped, and very few puddles blocked my path. The bat thwacked against leather stitching, and Tyson raced for home, head up, arms pumping. It would be close. He slid again, this time colliding with the toes of the catcher, red mud streaking the back pockets of his white baseball pants. He sprang to his feet, brushing off the front of his uniform.

"Safe! Safe!" I screamed, high-fiving the family carting folding chairs into the park. "Woohoo, Cubbies! Way to get dirty, Tyson!" He tipped his hat to the stands, his wide grin visible from the outfield, then ducked into the dugout. I hoped Keith had caught it on camera.

"Was that your son?" a bystander asked, arms draped over the outfield fence.

"Yes, yes it was," I beamed.

"You must love this."

I looked down at Cade snuggled comfortably against my chest, his face serene. His fingers wiggled when I replaced the blanket. Keith jogged to my side and kissed my cheek.

"I do," I said. "I've waited forever for this."

## Questions for the Reader:

*What do you do to replenish yourself, to refill your tank?*

*What do you do for downtime?*

# A Birthday Present

Slices of half-eaten pizza and wadded-up, oily napkins littered the table. Only a few people still occupied the seats. All the little ones had long since abandoned dinner to go play games. Tyson squealed behind me, feverishly pressing the buttons and levers and ignoring the direction to insert two tokens to play. He loved the pirate-cove game, firing cannons at Davy Jones' ghost army. I knew Grandma Karen would keep a close eye on him.

I crossed my legs and reached down to check on Cade. His raven head slumped sideways in his carrier, his pudgy cheeks cushioning his slumber. Every once in a while, his eyes flickered at a siren blaring for the latest jackpot winner, but he would sigh and lower his chin back down to his chest. I never tired of looking at him. I couldn't imagine my world without him. At the other end of the table, Keith reminisced with Grandpa Cal about fishing at Flaming Gorge, leaving me to fend for myself.

I sat next to the car seat and fiddled with my phone, passing the time playing Solitaire. I shut it off when I heard footsteps coming toward our table. I took a deep breath and ran my fingers through my hair. Josie reached the table, then straddled the bench on the other side in a pair of fitted denim overalls and a striped, orange halter top. She swatted at the stiff black locks on her shoulder threatening to stick to her lip gloss. I knew agreeing to meet for a reunion in Utah four months after Cade's birth might be awkward. We were still new at this. I tried to ignore the platform stilettos she'd chosen to navigate the kids' arcade in.

"Hey, sorry I'm late," she announced.

I tucked my phone back into my purse and smiled. "No problem. I'm glad you made it. How are you?"

"Can't complain." She searched the room. "Where is everyone?"

"They're off playing. Have you had anything to eat?"

"Yeah." She scanned the room, barely listening. When she didn't see anyone she knew, she sat down and rummaged through the purse on her lap. She found a pen and wrote a note to herself on her hand.

"So, how is work going at the café?" I asked.

"Hmmm? Oh, it's not bad. Mom agreed to keep me around, and it worked out for her to be my guardian for now."

I glanced down at the chunky electronic bracelet clasped around her right ankle. A small light flashed intermittently. She wore it proudly, even rolled up the pant leg to show it in full view. "Is it hard having that thing on?"

"No, but I hate having to check in with someone all the time. I'm doing good."

"Your mom says you've been attending a support group."

"Yeah, I've been clean for about a year now. Hardest year of my life with having the baby and all. The first time, I didn't know what was going to happen. I wasn't with it. This time, sober, you know, I felt every emotion. Every pain. Every hurt." She paused and bit her lip, her large hoop earrings brushing her shoulders. "In a lot of ways, he saved my life, you know." She nodded toward Cade. "I guess I had to really smack bottom before I could pick myself up."

I nodded. No one had ever disclosed what "rock bottom" meant for Josie or the details of her most recent charges. Grandma Karen had shielded us from the darkest parts of her daughter's rebellion. We only knew about her recovery successes. "We've been really proud of you."

"I'm proud too. I never thought I could get this far. In a month or so, my goal is to move into the halfway house to be closer to my support group."

"That would give you a little more independence."

"Yeah, and I would still be around some of the girls."

I didn't know if that was a good or bad thing. "What do you want to do after?"

"Dunno. Haven't thought much about it." She picked up a cold piece of pizza and tore off a slice of pepperoni. She slipped it into her mouth and grinned, the small gap between her front teeth showing. "Oh!" she gasped and smacked the top of her legs. "I got somethin' to tell you." She leaned toward me conspiratorially.

Curious, I leaned in, following her lead.

"Nobody knows," she said, tenting her hands over her mouth. "Well, no, that's not true. Randi knows, but no one else." She looked around like a giddy preteen.

I expected her to dramatically show off her left hand, dangling her fingers to display a breathtaking diamond. I nodded stupidly. Was there any doubt? I'd probably clap my hands, my breath catching in my throat. I'd wrap my arms around her, squealing an octave above my normal voice, "Congratulations! You guys will be so happy together!" Then I'd see that sparkling gemstone and ask if they'd picked a day.

Her giddiness was contagious. I felt myself growing antsy for the big reveal.

She covered her lips with her fingertips and giggled, bursting with joy. She looked around her. "I'm expecting," she mouthed, gently patting her perfectly flat stomach.

"You're what?" I caught myself, not wanting my tone to give me away.

"Ben doesn't even know yet." She cradled her belly, casting a backward glance at Keith and Grandpa Cal. "I figure I'll be due around late February, early March. Maybe this time we'll give you guys a daughter."

*Oh no. No, no, no. Is it even possible so soon?* "Congratulations," I squeaked out halfheartedly. I stared at her. My phone clattered into my lap, and I clasped my hands together to hide the shaking. My mind raced, trying to think of an additional response.

Oblivious, she grinned and bounded away, grabbing the paper cup of tokens Grandma Karen had bought for the kids. "I've got to get in on this." She raced over to Tyson, now at the basketball games, and began to shoot the loose balls into his hoop.

I poked at the salad on my plate, my appetite gone. I dropped my fork and rubbed my eyes, looking down the length of the table at Keith, then busied myself with packing the diaper bag and the penny treasures Tyson had won. Cade raised his head, rubbing it back and forth in his chair, his tiny lips rooting for something other than the corner of his blanket. I pulled him into my lap, recalling a moment at the beginning of summer when a famished little Cade had howled for a bottle in the back of a baseball wagon.

I had tugged on the wagon handle, pausing to take big gulps of air as sweat trickled down my face. The sand squished between my heels and my flip-flops, making it impossible to get traction, so I kicked off my shoes, praying my bare feet wouldn't find a shard of glass or an ocean creature waiting to sting me. I tried to ignore the stares around me. I thought I'd been ingenious bringing the baseball wagon to the beach, but when the wheels sank deep into the sand, I knew I had been taken.

I remembered how Tyson had skipped around me, finding pieces of seashells and shoving them into the pockets of his swim trunks. Keith, stark white against the glare of the sun, hunched over, lumbering under beach blankets, umbrellas, sand pails, and everything that would not fit into the wagon. We stood out. We didn't have the stereotypical cameras slung around our necks or fanny packs around our waists, the baby carrier and Bumbo in the wagon having drawn tourist targets on our backs.

We spread out the quilted red-and-white-checkered blanket. I positioned the umbrella and wagon next to me and tipped a bottle up for baby. I made sure he was well shaded and cool. Keith dropped down next to me, smearing sunscreen on his arms, traces of white still on his face. "How am I doing?" he asked.

"Almost there. A couple of missed spots right . . . there. I got 'em." I rubbed at the white streaks on his nose and at his hairline.

He claimed one side of the blanket and said, "Ahh, let's stay here all day."

"I don't have any plans," I said. Though we'd grown up in the harsh desert, nowhere near a beach, we adapted easily to the seaside. It was my happy place, my paradise. I hugged my knees to my chest, then stretched out in the shade. I closed my eyes, feeling the cool sea breeze roll in. Tyson chased each receding wave out into the ocean and then ran away as the next wave pursued him to the shore. I could have stayed there forever.

I blinked, the dazzle of the arcade games coming back into focus. Once again, I smelled sweaty kid feet and cheap, burned pizza. I felt the loneliness of the abandoned chairs around me. I wanted to be back under the shade of that umbrella. I wanted to taste all the fruit samples at the seaside market and then have Keith tell me how amazing I looked in the Celtic-knot necklace I'd found at the craft boutique. I wanted sandal lines on my feet, my hair messy and free. I didn't want to think about another adoption. Not just yet.

*I'm expecting.* Those two words curdled my stomach. *Is Josie serious? Would she really think about placing a third child with us? Now that she's cleaned up her life, is she in a better place to care for a child? What will her family say? Will Ben want to have a family when she tells him?* I didn't want to think about the next few months, dreading the emotional roller coaster it might be.

But as I listened to the rhythm of Cade's satisfied slurps on the bottle, I let my mind wander. I shouldn't have. I didn't mean to. In my mind, I pictured a large brown box arriving on our doorstep, me reading a note on the side and gathering my family around it. We'd recruit our neighbors to film us opening it and releasing dozens of delicate pink balloons into the air. We'd scream and hug each other and our boys. Taped to the bottom, I might find an ultrasound picture and a little headband dotted with tiny mums. Our Solace. Our little girl. Maybe this is how she needed to find us.

I winked at Grandma Karen as she brought Tyson over to me, his pockets bursting with tickets. Josie appeared behind him and thrust her open palm toward her mom. Karen sighed and drew out a crisp twenty. Josie's fluorescent fingernails snatched it, and she scampered away to play some more Skee-Ball without waiting for any children to join her. And then it hit me: *Yeah, I can hope for a box like that, but it's not going to happen. Ever. Josie's made some progress, but she's still got a teenager mindset. She's the center of her own universe.*

A massive lump pulsated in my throat as I hugged everyone goodbye. We waved as we drove out of the parking lot, both boys asleep almost immediately in the back seat. I gazed at the Wasatch Mountains outside my window, trying to make sense of my feelings. I filed some of those thoughts as *What if this is it?* and the others under *It's too soon to consider it.* Maybe even another category could have been *Don't go there.* I'm sure Keith wondered why I closed my eyes, strangely silent. Once again, my head pounded with each worst-case scenario. I sank sideways, leaning my head against the window. *I think too much.*

• — • — •

I knew she would call eventually. She had to. At first, I had hoped Josie would include me on the baby's growth and measurements. But she didn't. I expected a gender reveal in the fall, but nothing showed up in my mailbox or at my door. While Grandma Karen texted us "Merry Christmas! We love you," we heard nothing but eerie silence from Josie. I rationalized that she must have been extra busy and hadn't had a spare minute over the holidays. Or maybe she had just avoided me.

Since I hadn't heard from her in months, I figured she was struggling to form the words. In my anxious state, I knew what she might say: *I've been through a lot. Now that I'm better, I'm gonna to keep this one. We want kids. I'm sorry if I led you to believe something else.* I prepared myself to heartily wish Josie and Ben the best. And soon. With our foil "Happy Birthday" sign strung against the wall and a balloon bouquet bobbing against the air vent in the corner, it could happen anytime. Someone always called on birthdays.

Brinley's puppy body awkwardly sprawled across my lap, her head drooping off the side of the chair as I typed. I could feel the weight of her, the warmth against my stomach. Occasionally, she shifted and readjusted, wiggling into a softer spot, a barely audible whine escaping her mouth. I scratched her soft head, her flanks rising slowly with each breath. "Oh, Brinley girl," I teased. "How am I going to get this work done before Cade's party?"

She didn't raise her head at all. I didn't force her off. I enjoyed having her there. In a small way, I wondered if this was what pregnancy felt like. The movement. The kicks and twitches. The weight against my legs as I sat a little farther from the desk than I usually would. My phone sounded in my pocket, startling her. I said a silent prayer and pulled it out of my pocket.

"On my way," Keith texted. "Need me to pick anything up?"

I released the air in my lungs. "Nope, good to go," I texted back.

I set it facedown on the counter while I rounded up the eggs and cake mix. The beaters spun the batter into smooth chocolate, and I dabbed spoonfuls into the cupcake liners. I licked the spoon and set it in the sink. When my phone buzzed again, I hastily wiped my hands and turned it over to look at the number. Even though I didn't recognize it, I answered anyway.

"Hey," a familiar alto voice breathed into the line.

I tensed a little and sat down on a dining room chair. Tyson streaked by, weaving through the streamers taped to the counter.

"Josie, hi. How's it going? Is this a new number?"

"No, it's not my phone. I'm good. My mom just told me it was Cade's birthday."

"Oh yeah. Sure, hold on. Let me grab him. He's in the other room. I pulled Cade onto my lap and sat with him on the stairs. I held out the phone for him.

He nodded as Josie asked him about his special day. She laughed at the nonsense sounds he garbled into the phone.

I put it back to my ear. "Still no words yet. What's new with you?"

"Oh, nothing much. I've got my own place now."

"Really? I thought you had plans to move in with roommates at the halfway house."

"I did, but that was before Ben and I broke up."

"Oh, I'm sorry."

"Don't be. I'm with another Ben now." She chuckled.

"A different Ben? Well, that makes it easy to remember."

"I know, right?" She paused, suddenly done talking. I didn't know how to navigate the speed bump in the conversation.

"So . . ." I treaded delicately, "how has the new Ben adjusted to the new baby?"

"New baby?"

"Yeah, you know . . . you told me you were due a few weeks ago."

"Oh, that. Well, the old Ben and I were talking awhile ago, and he wasn't sure he could do another adoption. Since his birthday was coming up, I just gave him an abortion for a birthday present."

"Oh." I slumped onto the bottom stair, my back against the wall. I felt like I had just been slapped. Hard. I reached up to my face, feeling the skin around my eyes. I couldn't think. Shame on me for hoping too hard! As I propped my feet up against the railing, she landed another blow.

"I know. I wasn't sure if I wanted to go through with it this time, so I waited a little longer than normal. I'm pretty sure it was a girl."

"I'm sorry," I coughed out, tears pricking my eyes.

"Don't be. I'm better off anyway. Well, tell the little guy happy birthday. I've got to go."

"Thanks for calling." I ended the call and let the phone slip from my fingers. It bounced on its rubber case and landed face-down on the tile. *Breathe.* My gasps rolled out one after another, and I gripped the railing of the stairs, my other arm clenched around my stomach. The room spun, and I whimpered, not able to get enough air to inflate hope into my body. It was a girl.

I tried to avoid visions of my Solace's silent little face dumped into a garbage bin outside a sterile medical facility. I couldn't. On a day when I had cupcakes in the oven and birthday streamers taped to the kitchen counters, all I could think was that Ben had ordered a hit on a helpless little girl for his birthday. Maybe he'd enjoyed a slice of chocolate cake to celebrate.

## Questions for the Reader:

*Is there anything negative or toxic in your life?*

*What can you do to eliminate or lessen the effects?*

# Someone Is Missing

It started as I ran on the treadmill and heard a little voice call out to me when no one was around. I chalked it up to the whir of the belt as I tromped to a rhythm in the darkness of a cold basement. Occasionally, I set the table for dinner, placing five plates instead of four. Then I'd gather the extra utensils and place them in the corner for another time. When asked about my family, I slipped once and said, "Three. I have three children." I never did track down the stranger to correct my mistake.

The idea germinated in conversations with my siblings. Nick had two kids. Marie had three. The debate began when they claimed that going from two to three children was harder than any other transition because you had to go from "man-to-man" to "zone" defense. I desperately clamped my mind shut on the idea of having more children. After over a year's worth of heartache following Josie's fateful happy-birthday call, I'd reverently and permanently filed Solace away into a special niche of my memory.

But without warning, her porcelain face would pop into my mind no matter how hard I tried to prevent it. I tried to talk myself out of it. I rationalized that the searching hurt too deep, that the process would tax and threaten my young family. And yet, there she was. Like so many other times, she'd locked her bewitching eyes on mine, wondering why I ran away from her. Life was good, though. We were comfortable with the status quo, and so I wished her well and carried on.

• — ● — •

It was just an average Tuesday night as I squatted behind the plate, a sorry, inexperienced catcher, my mitt too stiff to close. Tyson dragged his lumpy baseball bag behind him, his batting gloves hanging out of his dusty back pocket. His recent growth spurt had left his pants showing more sock than usual. Cade clambered onto the bag, arms and legs clenched around the sides. He hopped off to drizzle the dugout bench with his water bottle. Keith stretched his arm and tossed a couple of sliders into the fence to warm up. Tyson popped a shot to the infield, and Brinley's four little legs beat Keith to the ball. We all laughed as the determined black dog chased Tyson around the bases, slobbery ball in her mouth, making him stumble. Park joggers stopped at the fence, their fingers poking through the chain-link squares, to watch our little family game.

The idea that someone was missing swirled around me like the puff of red dust that came off my glove as I caught Keith's fastball with a thunk. I warred within myself. A family of four was a nice round, even number, perfect for most hotel rooms and buy-one, get-one deals. We fit comfortably into a midsize sedan, as Tyson's team made a name for itself in weekend baseball tournaments all over Vegas. To make matters worse, our adoption agency had closed its doors for good.

But, like a restrictive pair of new jeans, I needed time to get used to the possibility. I needed to try the thought on, wiggle around in it, stretch a little, see how it felt around me. At first, I sat on the thought, a little miffed that God would expect so much after all we'd been through. *Would it even be possible?* I analyzed it from every angle. Every what if.

I eventually called a truce with myself and agreed to a non-committal orientation with the Nevada Department of Family Services (DFS), nothing more. Keith and I sat in swiveling armchairs that dipped excessively when I leaned back. I reached for his hand, careful to avoid brushing my clammy nervousness against his palm. One couple after another squeezed in around a twenty-foot-long table, and before long, an additional ring of latecomers stood behind us with arms folded. A brusque, heavyset woman with an animal-print blouse and musky perfume frantically handed out stapled copies of DFS requirements for foster-family licensing.

I jotted a few notes in the margins of my paper, circling phone numbers and copying email addresses. Keith and I exchanged wide-eyed glances when they aimed a laser pointer at the statistics on how desperately children needed foster homes. The truth was in the numbers. Maybe some of those kids could use a forever home.

I'd heard of foster-to-adopt programs and the tragic situations where a biological parent simply wasn't in the best position to raise their child. I thought back to our neighborhood park. Our foursome could use a few outfielders, maybe a better catcher. *It could work. It might work.* I would hope that one day, the park lappers would see our foster-blended crew and whisper amongst themselves, "My goodness, that's an amazing family!"

I got so carried away in my reverie I could smell the freshly mowed grass in the outfield. That is, until the animal-print woman pounced on the answer to a question I had missed. "If a child is not returned to their biological family, we consider ourselves failures." Her index finger tapping against the desk emphasized her statement.

I frowned, rolling the words over and over in my mouth and not liking the bitter taste. *If a child is not with biological family, anyone or anything less than that is failure?* I fully understood the goal of foster care and could work with that. But what if? What if a judge ruled a parent incapable of caring for a child? What if they habitually chose their addiction over their offspring?

A woman in purple velour yoga pants raised a spangled hand, asking about the foster-to-adopt program.

"We don't encourage adoption at all. Our focus is reunification. Like I said, new family units are failures in our book," the animal-print lady answered decidedly.

I balled up the orientation paper and banked it off the wall and into the garbage can on the way out.

· — • — ·

I eased down the road, watching carefully for Raven Lane, a turnoff I usually missed. I could hear the click of the Gatorade cap and satisfied "Ahh" after Tyson swallowed the last gulp. He slammed the door and paused to give me our signature "I Love You" sign on his way to batting practice. I glanced at the building next door. "Orange Grove: A Private Foster Agency." I had no idea private foster agencies existed. I wondered how they operated in relation to DFS. Was their licensing process the same? What was private foster care? I drove home, determined to do a little digging.

In the fading light of the living room, I burrowed sideways into the slip-covered chair, my bare feet crossed over the edge. I could still smell the slightly burned scrambled eggs from our breakfast dinner as I pulled up the Orange Grove website. I grimaced at the flashing red advertisement offering a sign-on bonus of $1,000 for new foster families. Never mind the somber photo of a displaced young man trying to keep up with his homework on his own. Only five seconds on the computer and something didn't feel right. Coupon incentives and bonuses? Disappointment surged through me. But regardless of their recruiting tactics, they had serendipitously scheduled an open house in one week. I wanted to talk with them face-to-face.

• — ● — •

I drove past the turn for the batting cages and parked next to a single, purple-castle bouncy house, spires jiggling in the breeze. Cade gleefully skipped into the structure and bounced from one wall to the next, throwing his body weight forward and backward and finally landing on the bulging floor, breathing heavily. Tyson picked off chunks of his chocolate chip cookie, licking his fingers and washing them down with a lukewarm water bottle.

A woman with hair pulled tightly into a bun at the back of her head met me at the front door. Two folding tables filled every blank space in the small waiting room. The colorless, pictureless walls stared coldly at me as I perused the papers lining the tables. I grabbed a few and leaned against the doorframe, scanning the information.

"Do you have any questions about Orange Grove?" The woman approached, slipping a business card under my fingers.

"I've actually only driven by and noticed your sign. My husband and I have been to the foster-care orientation at DFS, but we don't know anything about private foster-care agencies."

"This is a higher-level-of-care foster agency. We specialize in finding foster families who can support children diagnosed with significant mental health issues. These are children who need more TLC than the average foster child. All of our children have a team of counselors and therapists."

"So, they don't go through the state? I'm confused. How do they come to you?"

"When these kids are removed from their homes, they are evaluated to determine their needs. The severity of their home situation is assessed. If DFS determines that the child requires a higher level of care, the state refers them to us. We offer additional training and resources to assist our parents with the children in their homes."

I peeked at Tyson out of the corner of my eye and watched for Cade's black hair bobbing up and down inside the bounce house. We already navigated the daily, uncharted course of learning disabilities, speech therapy, and homework. We had hired tutors and attended behavior-therapy support groups. We regularly met with principals and school counselors. A higher level of care with an already full plate? That didn't sound like a good fit.

The woman followed my gaze and tapped the paperwork in my hand with the tip of her inky pen. "You call me if you decide you want to move forward."

*I think she knows.* Maybe years of watching parents struggle with the psychological and emotional issues of foster children had softened her to what I felt. It was too much. Way too much. While I wished I could help them all, I couldn't realistically take on a foster child with such extreme needs. Not now.

I found a square of shade next to the flat-faced building and leaned against it. Blissfully ignorant of the sweltering heat, Cade squealed as Tyson shed his shoes and crawled inside the bouncy house. Occasionally, I could see a bony joint brush the sides of the castle, the whir of the air machine drowning out my endless trail of thoughts. I sighed. I still didn't know what our next step should be. Resigned, I gathered the boys and walked to the car, folding the pamphlets in half and tossing them on the passenger seat.

• — ● — •

I tried Catholic Charities Adoption Agency twice, leaving both email and phone messages. Nobody responded. I tried one a last all-or-nothing call. This time, a cheerful male voice answered, "Catholic Charities . . . Adoption."

"Hi, my husband and I are looking into options to add to our family. We saw that you have a monthly orientation, and I was wondering if we could stop by to learn a little bit more about your processes."

"Sure. Do you mind me asking about your situation?"

"We have two boys, both adopted, ages nine and two. It's hard to explain, but we feel like someone is missing. We've attended a couple of orientations so far and are just deciding on which agency."

"Who have you met with?"

I was unprepared for such a direct question. "We went to the DFS orientation and Orange Grove."

"Do you want to add to your family?"

"Yes, yes, of course we do."

"Then why are you looking at foster care? Look, let me just say this. The goal of foster care is to reunite children with their biological families. The goal of an adoption agency is to create new ones."

I could feel myself nodding along. "No, I know, but the cost—"

"—is not an issue if you have a plan in place. We help with that."

"I know, but . . . I just don't know if we can do that again. Emotionally or financially."

"Why don't you stop by on the twenty-fifth? We can answer any questions you might have."

I hung up the phone, somewhat hopeful for a change.

At the end of the month, Keith and I pulled into the parking lot, mouthing to the attendant, "Catholic Charities Adoption."

He waved us to the far corner of the building complex and the only free stall in the entire lot. I hopped out of the car, locking the door behind me, hoping the unshaven men standing around the fence didn't notice. I wasn't sure if they loitered, ready to pounce on us for our spare change or if the next meal in the cafeteria wasn't ready yet. Keith put his arm around me and guided me inside. A blond man who could have been Keith's doppelgänger in too-baggy khakis met us at the door.

"Are you the Barlows?" he asked. "I'm Nate, the adoption coordinator here. We spoke previously."

"Yeah, that's us." My phone sounded, and I fumbled to turn the sound off as my cheeks reddened.

"Weezer? Nice. One of my favorites."

I liked Nate already. It seemed weird to sit at a desk with a slideshow presentation when it was just the two of us, but it must have been routine. As we chatted about background checks and home studies, a fire alarm sounded, and we looked searchingly at our host. He led us outside, the summer heat oppressive as we crowded next to the bushes farthest from the building. The tedious process of clearing out a social services building stretched for more than half an hour. I dabbed my forehead with my shirt-sleeve. Once we received an enthusiastic thumbs up, we hurried back to the air-conditioned conference room, but as soon as we sat down, the fire alarm sounded again . . . and stuck. Nate shouted introductions to the agency's director, and we yelled "Nice to meet you!" into each other's ears as if we'd met at a Def Leppard concert.

For fifteen years, Keith and I had witnessed a pattern of bad omens proceeding the good decisions in our life. We knew we had found our adoption agency.

• — ● — •

I opened my scriptures, lifting the ribbon bookmark from where I had left off. It had become a habit now, a daily devotional of sorts. I began with a question, something that bothered me or weighed heavily on my mind. As I prayed in the morning, I brought the question up in my prayer and talked to God about it. I never actually audibly heard an answer, but I knew somehow that if it was important to me, it was important to God.

After I prayed, I wrote my question down and read my scriptures. As I read, I thought specifically about my question and looked for ways it could be answered through the words of God's chosen prophets. Some days, a line or two stood out to me. I highlighted those. Other days, unrelated thoughts came into my mind, and I wrote them down.

It was always funny to me that I didn't feel worried about the adoption. Or, better put, I wasn't fixated on it. Three times around, I knew the process well. I knew what to expect. I also had two little ones who grabbed my pinky fingers, leading me out to draw chalk pictures on the driveway. Their routines consumed my time and energy. The lack of free time sucked away the need to stew about everything that could go wrong.

But the face of adoption had changed significantly. When we'd adopted Tyson, we'd turned in our paperwork, sat back, and waited for the agency to call us. That wasn't the norm anymore. Self-marketing strategies now fueled successful adoption placements. Adoptive families networked their own contacts to find a possible matches. That bothered me. *How can we network and bring awareness to our situation?* I wrote my question down.

The more I thought about it, the more I was drawn to a particular scriptural account of a nation in bondage. They knew where God wanted them to be; they just didn't know how to get there. Without His help, there was no way they could escape their oppressors. I could relate.

In the story, the people met together in a council and presented different strategies, then formed a plan using all their resources and abilities. All of them. I paused and reread it slowly. That was it! My heart thumped inside my chest so forcefully I thought it was relocating to the right side. *Make a list of resources, contacts, talents, and abilities.* I frantically scribbled down the rush of ideas. I couldn't wait to talk to Keith. I called him midmorning.

"Hey, what's up?" he asked. I could picture him behind his big desk in what was once the storeroom. Boxes still lined one wall, the contents labeled and dated hastily. Though he had been in his office awhile, his pictures and diplomas still leaned against the side of his desk, obscured by the plant that wavered between dead and alive on the table. His Charlie Brown desk ornaments now watched him answer the phone, cutting into his billable hours.

"I'm sorry," I answered. "I know I'm a little early. You got a sec?"

"Yeah, sure. I'm just finishing up a brief, but I could use a break."

"So, I've been thinking about how we're going to help this adoption go through. You know, from a marketing standpoint." I cringed at the word *marketing*.

"And?"

"And I had kind of a special moment during my devotional this morning. Just wanted to tell you about it. I even have stuff written down."

"Okay, shoot."

"Remember the Andersons from our first adoption classes?" I pried.

"I guess so."

"Remember how they printed business cards with their family's info and handed them out everywhere, like, even in doctors' offices?"

"Yeah, so?"

"I know marketing our family is even more important now than it was then, but I could never be that bold. I could never go door-to-door. In my devotional this morning, I felt like I needed to make a list of all our resources, talents, and contacts. I started writing stuff that's doable for me—anything that will get the word out that we're adopting without being pushy." I could feel my excitement trickle into the phone line. "Will you brainstorm a little more with me?"

"Buggy, that's a great idea." He paused, lost for a moment. "You know, as you were talking, I was thinking about the old agency. I know Family Services doesn't perform adoptions, but they still offer counseling for families considering adoption and for single parents. Maybe they will point us to any resources we haven't considered."

"I hadn't thought of that. I guess to build on that, how about if we meet with our bishop as a reference for our paperwork? He has connections with a lot of people—other church leaders, even. He may know of someone considering adoption."

"It's a long shot, but it's worth a try. I'm writing these down. What else have you got?"

I looked down at the half-cursive list in front of me. "I guess the biggest, most obvious one is probably the hardest. We need to tell our families. Our friends and neighbors already know more about this adoption than our parents and siblings. It should probably be the other way around."

"Do you think it's time?"

"I don't think there's ever a great time." When I thought about telling them, I felt the same wave of nausea I did when the nose of an airplane dipped in turbulence. Two Christmases ago, my feminist siblings had degraded my decision to be a full-time mom. They'd refused to believe I had chosen so little for myself. They'd lectured me for not aspiring to more. They were wrong. I knew it then, but the argument concluded after they'd thought they had won. "No, we have to. We may not have their support, but it's better than everyone finding out another way."

I could hear Keith slowly exhale. "Okay, I'll call my side on the drive home tonight. We're headed home in a month; we can tell the rest of them then."

"I'll tell everyone on my side on Sunday."

Keith paused for a moment. "What about our baseball family?"

"Baseball family?"

"Yeah, you know, all the people we've met over the years. We probably know at least a few people from every team in the league. Even more when you count club ball."

"What about them?"

"Have you ever connected with any of them on social media or just at the games?"

"Just at the games. I don't have time for social media. Are you kidding?"

"What if we made time?"

I snorted.

"For just a certain amount of time every day, we could add and follow people we know through baseball. The same goes for church and school. We could put adoption updates on there, you know, to keep us fresh in everyone's minds."

As a stay-at-home mom, I'd figured I couldn't contribute much to self-marketing campaigns, but after stepping back and looking at the people we regularly interacted with, the names piled up. I could hear a garbled voice in the background and shuffling as Keith cupped his hand over the phone. "Was that Fran?" I asked.

"Yeah, she had a question about the calendar next week."

"I'll let you go. Thanks for letting me bounce some ideas off you."

By the end of the evening, we'd committed to mentioning our adoption in everyday conversations to build a network of people who knew we were hoping to adopt. Our dentist began to ask me about it each time we went in for a cleaning. His assistants seemed to know to schedule additional time to discuss the adoption. I dusted off the old family blog and polished it with updated pictures. I registered for online adoption sites, plugging in our information with more confidence than ever.

One by one, we checked each item off our list. Our friends at the park shook our hands, wishing us well and promising to let us know of any leads. I grew our social media each day, adding friends and followers to bulk up our lists. I composed a message to blast out to every family member, neighbor, church member, baseball player, teacher, business associate, study group, and school friend we'd ever had. If it were a movie scene, my finger would have hovered over the send button as the dramatic music crescendoed in the background. I never sent it. My phone rang instead.

## Questions for the Reader:

*We can't always change our situation, but we can choose how we respond. If you are struggling with something right now, what can you do? (Triage your priorities. Think in practical, bite-sized pieces.)*

*Sit down, write out your options. What support do you have? Have you prayed about it? What resources are available? Think outside the box.*

# Think of a Name on the Way

I'll confess there are some nights when we adjust bedtime forward a little to accommodate *Dancing with the Stars*. It's the same tactic parents use on New Year's Eve to fake the midnight hour as the ball drops on Times Square. When all is quiet, I tuck a packet of peanut M&Ms into the pillows stashed next to me and prop my feet up on the arm of the love seat. Keith swirls a little bit of root beer into his vanilla ice cream. Hand in hand, we critique the foot placement and musicality of the contestants—our non-date date night every Monday. This was not one of those nights.

Our new adoption caseworker, Dawn, called late Monday afternoon to announce that she had a "possible scenario." I stifled my exhilaration and bit my lip to keep my voice calm. I rummaged through the junk drawer, desperate to find a pencil without a broken tip or a pen with ink. I snagged a random piece of mail from the desk and bungled a few notes on the back with a green pencil. Contractually, Dawn had to read a script line by line. She detailed everything the agency knew about the child: physical health, developmental milestones, mental and emotional states, challenges, family background, and all hospital documentation. Everything but gender. Gender swayed decisions. Moving forward with an adoption should be based on situational facts, not on a deep-seated longing for a little princess.

Keith took the boys to bed. From the desk in the nook of the hallway, I could hear his spot-on Grover voice from *The Monster at the End of This Book*. The book quaked every time Cade mischievously turned a page. My sound effects weren't that advanced, but Keith's acting skills fell a little flat on *Green Eggs and Ham*.

I caught him skipping a page or two when he thought nobody would notice. "That Sam-I-am" had annoyed him for years, and he had tired of reading it long before Cade came along.

I yanked the bedroom door shut and reread the email Dawn had sent with the details of the "scenario." I ran my fingers over the edges of the chipped desktop and traced the blue permanent marker heart drawn on top. I brushed away at the dust behind the computer. With both elbows firmly planted on the desk, I propped my head against my fists. I shut my eyes and inhaled deeply, letting the air pass down my throat and into my chest. It swirled around inside.

*Heavenly Father, I feel pretty calm tonight. That's not like me at all. A few hours ago, Dawn called us about a child who matches our preferences. It's a big deal. It's hard not to get excited. A yes could mean we are suddenly parents again.*

*I'm not worried about the substance exposure. We've dealt with that before. But we don't know anything at all about the biological father. Very little about Mom. The agency is just guessing at ethnicity. But the baby is healthy and thriving. I can see us moving forward with this.*

*Please let us know if this is what we need to do. Is this child meant to be part of our family?*

My shoulders relaxed as I released a cleansing breath into the dark niche. I swiveled on the desk chair to look at the pictures on the wall: Baby Tyson with the same expression as his stuffed animal. Baby Cade in a U of U jersey, held on a lawn chair by Tyson in the rival BYU blue. Keith in a scarecrow costume. Me in my senior photo, sunburned and blistered. Me in pigtails and overalls on the tire swing at the cabin.

I missed that cabin. It bordered the Provo River, and I loved hearing the currents roar against the banks in the middle of the night. I remember crouching at the edge, dipping my fingers into the freezing water. I would stretch farther, rubbing the palms of my hands against the smooth stones poking out of the rapids. I could still feel the peace of it all—the mountain air on my face, the cool slickness of the rock in my hand, the deafening rush of water. My heart hummed. Contentment filled my little space.

For just a few minutes, I allowed myself to imagine. Our baby girl names had been "taken" many times over by family members ignorant of our claim to them. First come, first served. That's how big families operated. I pulled up a website brimming with proper baby names for our Solace. I scrolled through the lists, testing the sound of each one on my tongue.

After ten minutes, I shut the laptop and snuck down the staircase. I had a feeling Dancing wouldn't happen, but I needed my M&Ms to get through the night.

•　—　●　—　•

I slept well, anchored in knowing God understood the decision to be made. Keith rolled onto his back, pillow partially covering his face. My claustrophobic tendencies to shove away anything from my face made it difficult to see him that way. I watched his chest rise and fall, his body engulfing the diagonal of the bed. Whenever he was out of town for work, the blankets barely wrinkled. Any other time, they twisted, knotted, and slipped off the edge until morning, when I kicked free of my fetters.

Our late-night discussion lingered between the two of us like the smell of homemade bread long since pulled out of the oven. I longed to shake him awake. And yet, face-pillow aside, I enjoyed watching him sleep. No one could sleep like Keith. As if on cue, his eyelashes fluttered and he stretched and lifted the pillow off his face.

"Morning, love," he slurred.

"Morning, Buggy. Sleep well?"

"Yep, just not long enough."

"How are you feeling this morning?"

"Pretty good."

I waited for more. It didn't come. "So, what do you think?" I asked impatiently, clearing all pillows away from him.

"I don't know. Same as what we discussed last night. How about you?"

I thought back to the ebb and flow of the day before. "I don't feel strongly either way. That's the problem. If this is something crucial for our family, I feel like I should probably feel different, but I don't. On the other hand, I don't feel bad about anything either."

"Then maybe the choice is ours."

"Maybe. So . . . we move forward? Should I call Dawn?" I asked, eyeing the phone on the nightstand.

"Probably ought to hold off until later. I don't think the office is open until nine."

I nodded and headed to the closet and chose a Chevron-striped shirt and a pair of jeans that puckered at the waistline. I threaded a peeling belt through the loops and tugged on a pair of Halloween socks. I combed through the tangles in my temperamental hair and let it fall naturally in waves around my ears.

I woke Tyson, who stumbled into the kitchen, his shorts and T-shirt scruffy but clean. His hazy eyes told me he'd had another rough night. His insomnia didn't seem to interfere much with school, but when it did, I would receive emails from teachers miffed that he'd snoozed through their lectures. He munched half of a "popper" seed muffin and slid his backpack onto his right shoulder. Once he met up with his buddies at the corner, he would perk up.

I reminded Tyson that we planned to call the agency and might need to pick him up early. He nodded without listening and sauntered out the door with a quick "I Love You" sign. I paused on the porch, suddenly nostalgic, smiling at the memory of the agency's frantic phone call the night before we picked up Tyson. I watched as he tucked his hands into the front pocket of his hoodie, his skater shoes inked with permanent-marker doodles. He was almost the same height as I was. Where had the time gone?

I looked at the clock. A quarter past eight. The office probably wouldn't open until nine, but I dialed anyway. To my surprise, a voice answered on the third ring.

"Good morning, Mrs. Barlow. We've been waiting to hear from you."

"Good morning, Dawn. How are you?"

"I'm great. Do you have any questions for me? Have you and Keith decided what you want to do with this scenario?"

"No, I don't think we have any questions. Some of the medical issues are a small concern, but nothing that is a deal breaker. I think we'd like to move forward and speak with the doctors a little bit if possible."

"So you're saying yes?"

"Yes, we are ready to do this!"

"Then congratulations! You are having a boy! He is actually here in the office right now. He was discharged from the hospital this morning. You'll want to hop in the car. Go ahead and think of a name on the way over so we can have the paperwork ready for you."

Leave now? A boy? I wasn't sure which to focus on first. Again, a boy. I loved boys. I had adapted to their strange sounds and innate ability to wrestle each other for no reason at all. However, I was absolutely positive, 100 percent, this time, that it would be a girl. *What is going on? Is this meant to be? We are looking for Solace!*

We could have requested a girl when we'd filled out the paperwork. My pen had hovered over the empty box a couple of times. But I couldn't do it. Before we turned it in, we'd discussed it again. *No, if God wanted us to have our little girl now, He would have sent us Solace.* It flashed in my mind that we would need to complete yet another adoption to find our little girl. Where was she?

I left the box of cereal on the counter and hustled Cade out to the carrying his socks and shoes. Keith called work. While I waited, I stretched my foot up against the dashboard, fumbling with my untied shoelaces, half of a granola bar hanging out of my mouth. I muttered under my breath. I pictured the dingy Converse footprint this would leave on the gray vinyl, then cursed myself for thinking such a dumb thing at a time like this. *Do I have everything?* I checked twice to see that Cade was buckled in behind me, only last minute remembering to toss in the smaller, extra car seat. We could install it at the agency.

I held Keith's hand over the console. We had about forty minutes. First item of business: name. We hadn't discussed boy names at all, but we'd borrowed the left-over short list from Cade's newborn days. Surely we could come up with something. We volleyed names back and forth, analyzing the strength, masculinity, cadence of each one. Too unique. Too overused. We felt like chess players at a major tournament, hitting the chess clock button after each move. The phone buzzed against my backside, and I panicked into the receiver. No, we hadn't decided yet! We countered a couple more middle-name possibilities and texted the twenty-minute masterpiece to the agency.

I dialed my mom and leaned my phone up against the dashboard. I never called my mom at work, so when she answered right away, I faltered. "Um, guess where we are."

Mom refused to play along. "I can't even guess. Where are you?"

"On our way to pick up your new grandchild. He was released from the hospital this morning." The silence filled the space of the car, riding on the hum of the tires as my mom contemplated my words. Was I joking? No, I would never prank anybody like that. I smirked as I measured the pause on the other line balanced with the laugh-out-loud whoop, probably inappropriate for the accounting office she oversaw back in Utah.

"You're kidding! Are you serious? You're serious."

"I'm serious." I swiped at the tears that seeped down my cheeks with the sleeves of my jacket. I had managed some eyeliner and mascara before we left, but I was sure both had trickled into brown smudges nestled in the creases under my eyes.

"And guess what?" I added.

"What's that?"

"It's another boy."

"A boy? Oh, wow, you're going to have your hands full. Have you tried dad? Did he answer?" Sometimes dad ran the heavy equipment on the job sites and couldn't hear his phone over the construction around him. Other times, he drove the dump truck and waited in the air-conditioned cab while the other workers loaded him up. That was the best time to catch him.

"No, I haven't tried. He's next," I promised.

"Well, keep us in the loop."

"I will." I couldn't remember the last time I'd giggled with tears swimming in my eyes. I acted so foolishly and giddily, but I didn't care. All those years of meticulously planning a pregnancy announcement or gender reveal! I had always wanted that. I would have been so creative. And here I sat, shoes half tied and snotty sleeves, providing the most powerful punch of a surprise I possibly could. Oh, how I wished this moment would last! I called my dad with the same result.

"Your turn, Bug." I dialed my mother-in-law and held the phone between us. A tired, cheerful voice answered.

Keith could barely choke out, "Hi, Mom," before he was wiping his wet face with his free hand. I stared at him, surprised. I could count on one hand the number of times I had seen him cry. It touched me that this moment ranked with the other major events. He looked at me, pleading, clearing his throat to gain control.

"Kathy, it's Chani. We're okay. We just have something to tell you." My voice cracked, and I knew my mother-in-law easily recognized the sounds.

"Is everyone safe?"

I laughed out loud. "We're safe. We're just—these are happy tears."

"Okay, take your time." It probably killed her to say those words.

Keith coughed and cleared his throat again, the emotion winning the battle each time. He finally mustered, "You're going to be a grandma again."

"Really? When?"

"Right now. Right now. We're on our way to the agency to pick up your new grandson."

• — ● — •

I knelt on our living room floor beside the baby, stroking his head, intrigued by his dark eyes. He wrinkled his eyebrows, studying me uninterrupted for the first time. He was beautiful. I would never know his full story. His anonymous family had respectfully wiped their names from all hospital records and refused any future requests for contact. His birth mother had her reasons for her request. It didn't bother me. There were no speed bumps, no hurdles, no last-minute surprises. If all adoptions were this smooth, everyone would stop saying, "I've always wanted to do that" and do it.

The front door opened, and Tyson scrambled inside. As always, he called out for me, but he didn't finish the last syllable when he saw the new baby on the blanket. He tossed his backpack and jacket on the floor and looked over his shoulder. A porch full of curious faces pressed in behind him. Tyson had obviously spread the word after we'd called him between classes.

"Hi, Snoog, how was school?" Keith shouted from the kitchen.

"Eh, it was school. Same as every other day."

"So, here he is." I held up the little boy for Tyson to see him better. "Your brother Hudson."

Tyson grinned. "Can I hold him?"

I placed the wiggling infant in his arms, and he strutted toward the doorway, proudly displaying his new brother to the masses. This spontaneous child must seem so strange to everyone else. In preschool, Tyson had assumed we just went to the hospital and picked out our favorite baby whenever we felt like it. For a while, he had struggled to understand that babies grew in mommies' tummies. Keith sat down on the couch, holding Cade in his lap. I winked at him.

"Tyson told us that he had a new brother, but we didn't believe him," one of the boys on the porch admitted.

"Yeah, we thought he was kidding. He bet us five dollars."

That sounded just like Tyson. A few extra bills were passed across the crowd and into his pocket. I ushered the group inside for a few minutes. A few of the boys hung back, arms crossed, looking to each other for guidance. A couple of the girls knelt on the blanket beside me, taking Hudson's tiny hand inside theirs.

"Oh, he's adorable!" they crooned.

Tyson grinned. "You know you can come back again anytime to hold my brother."

The girls looked at each other and smiled on the way out. He shut the door only to hear the doorbell chime. He opened it again, rolling his eyes, "Okay, what did you leave—"

My friend Jen stood on the porch, arms piled high with steaming pizza boxes and a salad bowl. "I didn't know what you liked, so I just got a little of everything" she said.

I stood to hug my friend and recounted a few of the details of our whirlwind day.

She handed me the stack. "I hope you don't mind, but I passed the message along to the bishop. I think he spread the word. A lot of people already know that you're home."

I thanked her and placed the boxes on the counter, the smell of garlic wafting through the house. I couldn't resist lifting the lid and sneaking a slice.

• — ● — •

I often wondered why I had felt the need to write down a battle plan, to strategically grow our social media accounts, to find community resources and learn to communicate openly with everyone about our adoption. I had thought that networking would lead to our adoption. But it hadn't. Hudson came anyway.

Our doorbell rang for days. Our baseball family brought us their hand-me-downs in big Trader Joe's bags. A church member sent over a practically new exercise stroller she no longer needed. Six months' worth of diapers and wipes from friends and family all over the country arrived at our doorstep. With all the freezer dinners, I didn't have to cook. I thanked God for the circle we had assembled who shared so generously and without being asked. I would need to lean on their support much sooner than I realized in the coming months.

One would think that by the third child, I would be used to the "newborn phase." But I wasn't. For the first couple of weeks, our support system buoyed us in our fight against a blurry, sleep-deprived existence. I powered through consistent headaches, still shuttling the boys to school, baseball practice, and doctor's appointments. Keith took over as much as possible after work.

But one day, Hudson began to whimper, a slow, churning protest down in his belly that worked up enough steam to wriggle up his throat. Then he threw back his head and screamed. His face blustery and red, he refused to cuddle against my cheek. His eyes squeezed out hot, angry tears that spilled down his cheeks and onto my T-shirt.

I bounced him a couple of times, stroking his head, his back, his belly, looking for the source of his pain. I swayed, hoping to lull him back to sleep. It only made him mad. I laid him down on the blanket, swaddling him and pulling him close, but he fisted his way through the folds to swat and kick at the air. I placed him in his swing, turning on music as he rocked gently. He refused. He balked. He wailed all afternoon, missing critical naptimes and ignoring mealtimes.

That evening, as Keith walked through the door, I handed him the bawling baby like a baton in a relay. I stepped outside, stumbling out into the crisp air on the walking trail behind our neighborhood. I hugged myself in my thin jacket, my frumpy shadow looking up at me in the setting sun. Embarrassed, I turned to go back. But I couldn't. I paused as I looked over the neighborhood below me, the baby's cries still ringing in my ears. I wasn't sure why, but I began to tear up too. "What am I doing wrong?" I asked no one in particular.

The days spun slowly as we tried changing formula while alternating sleeping and holding positions to avoid putting pressure on Hudson's belly. He screamed even louder. We massaged. We went for drives. Though he was probably too young for teeth, we checked his gums. We tried wrapping him tightly, then we tried loose. Nothing helped. The pediatrician could only recommend the things we had already tried.

I drooped onto the couch, a line of unwashed bottles crusting on the counter. I had managed to get out of bed, but only as far as the chair, before I collapsed again. The back of my neck ached, the incessant newborn shrieks stiffening my shoulders and settling into my temples. I flogged myself for not being enough for my son.

Helpless days dragged out into hopeless weeks. Sometimes I would place Huddy in his crib, the bedroom door shut tight, just to give myself a break from the screeching. Edgy and irritated, I allowed the boys to escape into TV shows—endless twenty-three-minute episodes of canned laughter interspersed with snarky teenage comments. I didn't care. I felt myself slipping and had no idea how to retain my sanity. Keith tried to give me breaks, but long days and the demands of work kept him away. Frankly, I felt inadequate, my self-worth unprepared for weeks of colic.

Gradually, I turned inward, saddened by my inability to respond to my son. I wore jammies during the day, my hair greasy and untouched by dinnertime. I didn't remember brushing my teeth. I stopped wearing makeup and had no desire to get out of bed in the morning, even when I had been awake for hours. I buried my teary face in my pillow each night, knowing I had to do it all again the next day.

I didn't need a specialist to diagnose my depression. I knew I needed help, but I couldn't explain my blues. We'd adopted. My body hadn't delivered a biological baby, so my hormone balances should have been pristine. I had no medical excuse for feeling like the worst person ever. I just did.

I had felt severe depression with all the adoptions but reasoned it away each time. With my first, I could attribute the blues to changing my lifestyle, my work. With the second, a lot of time had passed. I had forgotten how much the lack of sleep affected my aging body. Adjusting to our new home and job demanded my best. But the third time was harder than ever. The rush of darkness overwhelmed my senses, and I didn't care that I didn't care anymore. I turned my head and fell asleep again, the baby still wailing in the other room.

Looking back, I should have asked for more help. God had given me a list of supportive friends and family. Phone numbers. Resources. Any one of them would have come running. Why I initially kept my struggles to myself, I will never know. I should have scheduled an appointment to see a mental health professional. But I didn't. The stigma scared me. God blessed me with opportunities to reach out to Him, to allow others to reach out to me, but I didn't take them. Not right away, at least.

## Questions for the Reader:

*I know it's hard to ask for help. I would so much rather be the "giver" than the "receiver." How can you prepare yourself to accept help?*

*Is there anyone who might be able to help you right now?*

*Are you in a position to seek professional help or research community resources?*

# Find Her

Iknew it was officially Christmas when Keith pulled out his CD of a classic his Morrison grandparents used to play during the holidays. I hadn't been there, but could I picture an old turntable with black knobs next to a brightly dressed tree. The ornaments didn't match, but the fresh pine needles exuded an earthy winter perfume that filled the house. My vision melted into reality as the sounds of needle against vinyl warmed our own home into an inviting space so authentically Christmassy I perked up a little.

I thought I believed in miracles, especially at Christmastime. I'd experienced enough of them know God had sent me reminders of how much He loved me. I just had to watch for them. Angels, real and unseen, lightened my load and strengthened my capacity to endure the gray, dismal days. My sweet husband, my angel and best friend, never lost confidence in me, even during my rockiest bouts of hopelessness. He and a handful of my close friends pointed me toward the little glimmers of joy buried underneath hours of noxious howling.

And then it happened. One day Hudson started to cry and refused to stop. Then, two months later, he was done. He'd purged it from his system. It was my Christmas miracle.

When the wailing stopped, he began eating regular, hearty meals and sleeping through the night. As he slept consistently, my weary body slowly recovered. Without the screaming, we ventured outside. I'd bundle Huddy in a stroller in the morning, and we'd walk until we met the returning school bus. Each day felt a little better. My friends and family rallied around me, applauding both my mental and physical progress. The doubts in my clouded mind dispersed in response to the exercise, sunlight, and circle of support. My renewal didn't happen as suddenly as my son's, but it happened.

· — ● — ·

I fingered the clasp on the little mirror, trying to split it open with my fingernail. Soundlessly, it opened, and I bashfully peeked at my reflection, a work in progress. I cowered, knowing I had come underdressed, as always. The women around me had carefully applied thick strokes of mascara to their eyelash extensions. Freshly painted nails with ornate tips adjusted the buttons on their jewel-toned blouses. Maybe I'd missed the dress-code memo.

I turned to Tawnie, a quiet woman new to the neighborhood, and asked about her son's basketball season. She pulled out her phone, flipping through fuzzy pictures of a teenager standing at a free-throw line. Her eyes sparkled as she described the winning basket he'd scored in his last game and how he'd achieved triple-double status a few times this season.

The chatter ceased and the lights dimmed as a woman tapped the microphone. The host wore a cheerful yellow cardigan over a spring sundress, her voice high-pitched but welcoming as we kicked off the birthday celebration for the women's Relief Society chapter in our area.

I looked around the room. The ordinary gym was swathed in peach-colored lace and tulle, the elegant hues accented by long strands of tiny white lights. Old-fashioned vases with small electric candles adorned the centers of long, rectangular tables, small golden chains swooping from one candlestick to the next. The women crowded in, shoulder to shoulder, inching farther down, tighter and tighter, to make room for all the friends entering the room.

"Ladies, it is a pleasure to be with you tonight. Thank you for taking the time to spend this evening with us. As our servers bring out the first course, let me introduce you to Jane Welch, a marriage and family therapist from Southern Utah. Jane has five children and ten grandchildren, with another on the way.

"At the age of fifty-seven, Jane felt instinctively that she needed to pursue a graduate degree in psychology. It felt crazy to her, but she knew it was what she needed to do. It was her calling. With the help of her family, she finished her degree at the age of sixty and her doctorate by the age most people begin to consider retirement."

A short-haired, wiry woman with a sharp nose and extremely white teeth stood and moved to the front of the room. The gray scarf slung over her shoulders reached down to her waist and did little to hide her thin frame and flat chest. Her swooping skirt swished against the floor as she began to tell the story of why she'd pursued a new career so late in her life.

Impressed, I listened, picking occasionally at my spinach salad.

"I feel a special connection to women," Jane explained. "My empty-nester friends, the hairdresser, my nieces, all seemed to struggle with essentially the same problem. Not one of them felt like they were enough. They didn't measure up, especially when they compared their efforts to others' efforts."

The room hushed. Not one woman looked away from Jane.

She continued. "I had been there. I could relate to falling short of perfection. I had a unique understanding that was needed in my profession. God put me in a place to change lives if I was willing to listen."

She continued to talk about serving others even when the timing seemed wrong. I stared at my white porcelain plate, the remaining bits of chicken untouched. While the women who surrounded the table did not speak during the presentation, all other sounds faded into an indistinct haze. I fanned myself, suddenly over-whelmingly warm. In my mind, even Jane Welch's talking ceased and I felt, more than heard, an encouraging whisper. *Find her.*

I looked around the room, all eyes still on the gray mono-tone woman telling an anecdote about a fourteen-year-old in her office last week. *Find her*, the thought came again. I searched my mind for an explanation of this cryptic direction. I thought about my day, the people I'd interacted with, my boys, my husband. I retraced my steps to the grocery store, list in hand, writing down each of the totals as I placed the items in my basket. Nothing pro-vided me with the clarity I needed.

A face floated into my recollection, a tad dim and washed-out, perhaps, but still there, still familiar. I thought about the little girl with those piercing, light eyes, those dark lashes stark against her white face. I couldn't deny the earnest expression on her lips. Her dark, curly hair, exotic and beautiful, was tucked behind her ears. Again, the thought sounded forcefully. *Find HER.*

This time there was no mistaking it. My little girl, my Solace, had waited long enough. One would think such a direct impres-sion would send a more pious person to their knees, grateful for the heavenly nod. I shook my head, hot tears stinging my eyes. I picked up my plastic water glass and downed a few swallows, sputtering a little. A few ladies looked at me under their eyelashes, and Tawnie leaned over to ask if I was all right.

I excused myself and headed to the restroom, where I latched the stall door and paced as much as I could in the three feet of privacy. *Now?* I questioned. *Now?* I felt almost angry. *Hudson isn't even six months old. My family is happy. My family is settled. I'm good with where I'm at.* I fumed as I remembered that with each new child, I'd faced an intense fight to regain my mental health. But if I was honest with myself, I knew that the search for Solace would have popped into my subconscious at some point. Her face still haunted me occasionally.

Months ago, I had almost rear-ended the sedan in front of me when I passed a new billboard for Sunrise Children's Hospital. I'd pulled off to the side of the road and gawked at the little girl posed against a blue background. My breath caught in my throat when I looked at her eyes. *I know those eyes! That face!* My Solace stared back at me, larger than life, on the side of the road for all of Las Vegas to see.

I drove home, confused. *What is she doing on a billboard? Does she need a home?* I contemplated my next move. *Should I call Sunrise? Who would know anything about this little girl?*

I tried to explain the billboard to Keith. I even pulled up the marketing campaign online to show him the picture. He agreed it was her but shrugged when I asked him what I should do.

"Don't you think it would be creepy if you called just asking about that little girl?" he asked.

"Oh, I'm sure it would be. They would think I'm completely nuts. Or some stalker. Either way, there's no way they'll give me any information on her."

Over the next couple of weeks, I pulled up the picture online. I even took a couple of extra drives past the billboard. I knew there was nothing I could do, and so I dropped it . . . reluctantly. I convinced myself the actual little girl was simply a lookalike. The matter slipped slowly out of my consciousness, and I continued with my life without ever looking back.

Until Jane began talking about her career. Until I felt a powerful nudge to "find her." That billboard returned to my mind. Always the eyes. Those arresting eyes.

I remembered stories of the early pioneers of my church. Back then, men's names were read over the pulpit in front of the congregation for an assignment to serve a mission. They could choose either to accept or reject that opportunity to travel to foreign lands to preach Christ's words on their own dime. They left their families and employment to follow God's call to them as His missionaries. Whatever they chose, everyone would know.

I felt that way now. In that bathroom, one hundred feet away from rows of tables and women probably spooning the last of their cheesecake into their mouths, their white napkins crumpled in their fists, I felt their presence. Their scrutiny. Their judgment as to whether I would accept or reject God's call to find her.

I clenched my teeth, the muscles in my jaw working each line of defense that popped into my mind. I didn't have the stamina for another adoption process and trudging through grueling paperwork and background checks. Most of my friends were preparing graduation announcements for their children. A few shopped at thrift stores for wedding dresses they could tailor with lacy sleeves. I questioned whether I wanted more children at this stage of life. *How many years apart will the kids be? We tried to find her before, but she wasn't there. How fair is that?*

I splashed water on my cheeks, wiped them dry, and sighed. I plunked my purse onto the wet counter and dug for my keys, anxious for an excuse to leave. I couldn't sequester myself in a stall, so I crept past the doorway to the gym and waved a hasty goodbye to my friends. I tried to ignore Jane Welch and her divine calling to help others, following what God encouraged her to do. I slammed the car door and began to drive, oblivious to the streets I passed.

*What if I don't want to find her?* I challenged heaven. There were a dozen other women who would be much better mothers. *What if I am happy with the size of my family right now? God honors our agency and respects our choices, right? I'm fine. I'm my old self again. Keith's fine. We're adjusted to the baby. Why would we do anything to mess that up?*

I followed the street past the golf course, eyes brimming, accusing my Heavenly Father. I shouted until I couldn't think of anything else to say. When I finally got control again, I felt ashamed. I knew better.

## Questions for the Reader:

*Have you ever felt like you weren't enough?*

*What can you do to avoid comparisons?*

# Decisions and Setbacks

I'm the human version of Mentos and Diet Coke. My brain operates on extreme settings. When I felt the undeniable impression to find Solace, I'd exploded, spewing my venom all over the car, arguing with God. I reacted at Keith for not getting the boys to bed on time and ignored his apology until morning. Guilty and ashamed, I tried to patch together fragments of sleep through the long, troubled night.

I tried to reason the inspiration away, conjuring up every valid excuse to ignore God's direction. It wasn't logical. I couldn't understand. Why would He ask so much of me and my family? Hudson's seamless adoption process echoed in my head. The colic and my mental assault and recovery silenced it. How could I tackle something like that again?

But over and over, I reflected on an episode early in our marriage, well before we'd adopted Tyson. Keith and I had received our infertility diagnosis and procrastinated filling out the forms in the manila envelope next to the computer. I remembered feeling an unexplainable urgency to complete that paperwork. The tension had increased each day, though nothing around us had changed. But we waved the feeling away.

At the summit of my tension, my childhood friend had announced her pregnancy. She had ended a feuding relationship with her boyfriend and waffled between parenting as a single mom or placing the baby for adoption. We'd stood, barefoot in the driveway, listening to her discuss adoption as a real possibility. I could have opened up to her about our situation. At the very least, I could have shared some of the resources in the envelope. Sadly,

I never said a word. After that, the urgent feeling dissipated and regret surged inside me. I realized we had missed an opportunity. It would be another four years before we had another "at bat," and I didn't want to repeat that type of misstep.

I'd never been one who believed in making a decision and expecting other people to follow. Keith and I discussed things. Hours and hours of back and forth. And we took time to pray about things individually. And then, more discussion. We never made spontaneous decisions.

Early in the summer of 2017, we grabbed a couple of deli sandwiches and sat at a small table under a park pavilion. Hudson lounged in a jogging stroller at my knee. I unwrapped my club sandwich, handing Keith the extra red onions. The muted whistles of a soccer game mingled with the lights buzzing overhead.

"I don't know what to do, Bug. I want to do what we're supposed to do, but I feel forced," I tried to explain.

"We're never forced."

"That's just it. I know that. But adding another child to our family is not the course I want to pursue. The timing is awful."

Hudson babbled from the stroller and dropped his teething ring on the ground.

"What would be your first choice?" Keith asked, reaching down and handing it back to him.

I thought about it for a minute. "To be done. I want to be done with the baby phase and move on to the next. There's more options when the boys will be in school all day."

"You'd be great wherever you went. The billing office missed you when you left." He took another bite and swallowed, letting the silence between us linger a little longer than usual.

I ignored my half-eaten sandwich and twisted my short hair into a mindless braid, trying to slow down the back and forth in my head. I let the braid go and ran my fingers through it again. "I never told you, but I've been praying, well . . . about my purpose in life." I didn't know how to explain. It sounded so cliché. I risked an upward glance.

Keith nodded, his clear blue eyes encouraging.

I tried again, rubbing the pads of my fingers over the small crack on top of the picnic table. "In my accident, a lot of miracles happened. I probably shouldn't have lived, but I did. That's left me with an overwhelming sense of 'There must be something I need to do.' I want to find my purpose. I feel like it's time."

"What do you feel like your purpose is?"

I opened my Doritos and shoved a chip in my mouth. "If I tell you, promise not to laugh."

"I promise."

"It sounds too corny to say, but I really want to help people. I want to change lives." I unbuckled a fussy Hudson and balanced him on my lap.

"How would you do that? Would you go back to school?"

"Possibly. I've thought about it. I've thought, *Where can I make the biggest impact?* If I'd gone with my plan A back in college, I would be a physical therapist now. But that's not what I want anymore."

Keith winked across the table. "You should write. You've always wanted to write."

"Yeah, right."

His smile faded. "No, really."

"Eventually, maybe. But right now, I think I've narrowed it down. It would be an either/or decision. Either I go back to school or . . . remember the foster-care orientation we attended?"

Keith dumped his remaining chips onto the sandwich wrapper in front of him. "I remember. It wasn't the right time."

"That's it. It wasn't the right time then. But what if it's the right time now?"

He met my gaze, incredulous. "You mean you want to license through Nevada's DFS?"

"No, what if we looked into more of the private agencies?"

"What private agencies?" He balled up his sandwich wrapper and chip bag, tossing them into the garbage a few feet away. He put both hands in the air as his shot hit perfectly. He took Hudson into his arms.

"Nice shot." I stood, automatically scooping any remaining crumbs into my hand to toss as well. I held off on answering the question as I loaded the stroller with our half-empty drinks. "You wanna push?"

Keith took the handles, and I walked next to him, my hands shoved in my pockets.

"I caught a special news segment today. You know, those ones where they talk about community events?"

"Mmm-hmm." Keith pointed to a lizard on the sidewalk in front of us. We watched it skitter through the fence railing and down toward the brick wall.

"There's a Christian-based foster agency here that specializes in abuse situations. They were doing a fundraiser for children aging out of the foster-care system."

"Really? I didn't know such an agency existed." He stopped and turned to me. "What was the name?"

"Craig something. It was weird how I caught the segment. I never watch those things. It felt different." I was grateful I could look down at the sidewalk and not have Keith analyze my expression.

We took turns pushing the stroller, rounding the corners near the playground. Wild rabbits peered out of the holes in the rocks and scampered across the lawns. When we passed, they retreated a few feet away.

"I'm not even sure it's what I want to do. I guess I'm just throwing it out there, wanting to get your thoughts," I continued. "What if part of my purpose is to help these foster kids? What if this is how we find Solace?" I was on a roll. "What if this teaches the boys to serve others, to see the world beyond our little bubble?"

Keith shrugged. "It's something to think about, especially if you feel strongly about it. I'd like to meet them to find out how a private agency would impact our family. You know me."

I knew. It only took us a couple of years to buy a barbeque because of Keith's "analysis paralysis." By then, we had missed opportunities on two cycles worth of holiday sales. At one point, I'd just gotten frustrated and told him to pick one.

"Okay, let's think about it."

• — ● — •

The little black dog curled up against my chest, her soft head on my shoulder. I shut my eyes, letting her ears twitch against my nose. I could smell that distinct puppy smell as I nuzzled against her floppy ears. The weight of her body fit into the crook of my left arm, and I stroked her head, leaning against her, needing the comfort and warmth only a dog could give. "Oh, Brinley, how are we going to do this?" I whispered into her ear. Her eyes were shut, but she opened them slightly and tipped her head toward me.

I glanced down at my journal and read my latest entry:

*Church was remarkable yesterday. Instead of assigned speakers, the bishop invited anyone in the congregation to come to the pulpit and share their favorite scripture. He asked us to explain why it stands out to us. I had never seen anything like it before, and I wished Keith wasn't sick at home. I knew it would be a powerful meeting, but it was completely obvious when all three of my boys began acting out. I took baby Hudson out in the hall because he was crying. When I could hear my two remaining boys fighting (from all the way in the hall), it became a tap dance as to which kid needed to be removed and when. I did, however, catch one of the scriptures. One man mentioned a scripture about God's promises. His words did not impact me as much as seeing the story in the context of our situation. I felt strongly that this was a direct answer to prayer.*

*In the story he shared, the Lord prepares a land for His people. A special place. They have no idea what blessings await them. But to get there requires overcoming hurdles. More than that, He wants His people to trust Him enough to be able to do the impossible.*

*When I think about foster care, I feel like the story describes us right now. Like this is a path that could lead to our "promised land." Why? I don't know. We're comfortable with where we're at. But then again, so were the people in the scriptures. They had no idea what was in store. Neither do I.*

*God has promised his people tremendous blessings if we trust Him enough to take our journey in His cause. There will be opposition. It won't be easy. But this might be the next right step for us. (May 2017)*

I stroked Brinley's ears and set the journal down. It wasn't that simple. If we seriously considered foster care, it would take more than a manila envelope full of documents. We needed a new house.

I looked out the screen door at the giant brick wall behind our house. Tyson had perfected his pitch tossing one baseball after another at that wall. The faded chalk circle target sported dented and chipped bricks where he'd hit the mark. I thought of the boys in two of the upstairs bedrooms and Keith shaving in the mirror adjacent to our room. A foster license required a space for every child, and a little girl would need a room of her own. But we couldn't just add one. That was the problem.

And so it began. We pulled up realty websites and began searching for bigger homes with real grass in the backyard. We felt like the couples on HGTV, listing our must-haves and touring open houses. Secretly, I loved it. I visualized myself in one home after the next, checking off all my favorite features: crown molding, plantation shutters, French doors, stone countertops. When our house sold in two weeks, we knew we were halfway to our goal.

But our luck ended there. I lost count of how many homes we visited and how many offers we signed. A storm of rejections followed. We packed our duffel bags and moved into a Best Western in Boulder City and then an eight-hundred-square-foot rental. We had no choice. A muddled short-sale listing led us on for months, teasing us with all their added requests and greedy counteroffers. Trapped in a shady contract with half-truths forwarded back and forth between the Realtors, we waited it out. It wasn't meant to be.

Almost one year later, we closed on a home an hour north of our comfort zone. When we attended church the next day, I stood to introduce myself. I leaned into the microphone and confessed that I felt like our family had just completed a marathon to get there. I wanted to hug and high-five everyone and said as much. On my way back to my seat, I high-fived the guy sitting behind me. We were home!

God had orchestrated a move to a neighborhood well beyond our expectations. It wasn't just the stone countertops, square footage, or yard. We found ourselves only fifteen minutes from our foster agency and the epicenter of community resources to help license and prepare us for the next step of our journey. We didn't plan it that way. But a loving Heavenly Father needed us to be somewhere specific, even if we had to be patient.

## Question for the Reader:

*Have you ever received an answer to prayer as you read the scriptures or the words of the prophets?*

# Youth Harbor

Keith let Hudson climb onto his shoulders to see Cade's kindergarten class singing and clapping to "Don't Worry, Be Happy" at their graduation ceremony. I handed him a Spider-Man action figure and toyed with the camera on my phone to make sure I captured every swaying robe and tassel. After a celebratory pancake at McDonald's, I gathered the remaining threads of laundry day. I sorted whites, darks, bolds, towels, and lights, each pile always in the same place. Each load always in the same order. I could sort, wash, fold, and put away all in one day. I called it "Leave No Trace Laundry." If I managed my time efficiently, I could still make it happen.

My phone sounded in the kitchen, a pulsating sound that bounced off the black cabinets and textured backsplash. I gathered the straggling dirty socks off the floor from last night's Flash marathon and leaned against the washer as I checked my messages.

First, a text from Dinah at Craig Village. Dinah never called; she preferred texting to conversation. Or maybe she operated out of library "quiet zones" where they banned talking. "Nineteen children taken into Youth Harbor last night," the text read with a couple of photos of handwritten notes. "Male—age 2, Female—age 2" and "2 Boys—age 4." My heart beat a little faster. I looked over the list with Dinah's short tagline, "Siblings," to sum it all up.

Numbers on a page. No names. No identities. Orphaned, or at least temporarily displaced, and not even human. There was no way I could fathom pointing to a line item and picking out something to take home like a Cyber Monday sale. I bit my bottom lip, a bad habit the dentist seemed to bring up every time I visited.

It helped me to think, to cope. I frowned as I texted back, "Any more details?"

I started the washer and carried the laundry basket to my bedroom to fold the warm towels. "Can you come down?" she responded.

*Can I come down? Now? What will happen? Our foster license approval arrived only days ago.* I dropped an unfolded towel back into the basket and stared out the windows overlooking the pool in my neighbor's yard. The German shepherd looked up from his cushion and barked at me. *If I go to Youth Harbor, I will be able to see the kids in person. I'd know Solace's face anywhere. If she is there, I'll find her right away. Maybe even bring her home today.*

I evaluated my options. Because of the graduation ceremony, school had dismissed early. Cade licked Cheeto dust off his fingers while he and Hudson watched Looney Toons. Tyson could see himself home through the door. I texted Keith. The phone seemed to shrug right along with him. *Go ahead if you want.* I dropped my boys off at a friend's house down the street and texted Dinah. "I'm on my way."

I had never seen the inside of Youth Harbor, but I'd heard about it. We passed it whenever Tyson played in tournaments on the baseball field next to it. I was curious to see the temporary orphanage where children, once removed from their homes, were sent until social workers could find family members or foster families to take them in.

· — ● — ·

Dinah met me at the door and held it open as I walked inside. She smiled at me. "You ready for this?" she asked, her slight accent emphasizing the cadence of her words.

"I think so." I tried to interpret the sparkle behind her dark-brown eyes.

She motioned for me to follow, and I shadowed her through the security doors. "Candace's here too," she said over her shoulder.

I pictured the Craig Village agency director with her long, straight hair and easygoing personality. I had met her once during our classes but never one-on-one. "Oh, really? I didn't think Candace had anything to do with foster placements."

"Normally she doesn't. She pops in every now and then to check on things. This happened to be the day she decided to come."

I nodded, unsure whether I should feel intimidated or grateful.

Dinah led me to a small office hidden behind the fingerprinting booth. Candace waved as we walked inside, and gestured to a mismatched chair next to a circular table. Dinah tucked herself into the corner, pulling out a folded white sheet of paper with the same cryptic notes as the text. Candace unbuttoned the front of her suit coat and compared a stapled list of names, dates, ages, and hospital rooms. The two women scanned the synchronized pages, pointing to one name after another, understanding flashing across their expressions. Then they nodded and folded their hands on top of the papers.

"Last night, Youth Harbor took in nineteen new children," Candace began.

"I know. Dinah mentioned that. Can I meet the kids? Can we play with them?"

A woman with piercing brown rat-like eyes rapped on the open door. Her hair was caught up in a messy bun, her cheeks flushed as if she had just sprinted across the plaza. "No," she interrupted. "It's naptime. No one is allowed in the back. The kids are all down."

Dinah looked sheepishly at me. "I'm sorry, I should have told you the kids were about to go down for a nap. Maybe we can look at the lists."

I didn't want to look at the numbers again. I didn't want to see the parentheses stretching around two unnamed children, a desperate attempt to keep loved ones close, even if only through punctuation marks. I wanted to meet the kids. I wanted to roll them a ball and watch their eyes light up. I wanted to pose like Captain America and name off all the ninja turtles and impress them.

"I'm sorry, but due to confidentiality, we can't let just anyone back there right now," the flushed woman fanned herself with a few papers in her hand.

I looked across the table and met Candace's eyes, a pathetic plea for help.

"May we at least speak with the staff?"

I could feel her leveraging her authority as the head of the foster agency with the rat-eyed head of the children's ward.

The woman sighed to emphasize how inconvenient our request was, then nodded, walking well ahead of the group. As each door opened, the neutral paint faded, giving way to bright colors and shapes and dramatic scenes from faraway jungles and castles in fairylands. But even so, the cinderblock walls and double-paned windows felt like an abandoned but cheerily painted penitentiary. We crossed the courtyard, splashes of primary colors leading us from one building to the next. I didn't see a playground. No swings. No slide. No monkey bars. No rubber balls on the ground. Nothing that even hinted at children's play.

The beady-eyed woman scurried toward a staff of four women seated in folding chairs surrounding a single desk. They cross-checked clipboards amongst themselves. The banter stopped as we approached. The woman leading our group explained the reason for our visit. A Hispanic woman wearing pink rubber crocs rose and led me to a shelf full of plastic bins. Each colored bin had a polaroid of a child taped to the front, labeling a pair of lonely, but not lost, shoes inside. She pointed to the pictures. "These are the kids," she said with a halfhearted game-show-host gesture.

Dinah and Candace stood behind me, arms crossed. The women at the desk leaned forward to note my choice on their paperwork. I was now expected to pick a child not just based on an abbreviation but on a small polaroid and the condition of their sneakers. The pink-crocs lady stood with her hands on her hips, looking at the faces staring back at her from the front of each box. She began handing boxes to me. "Pick one," she seemed to say. I recoiled.

Panicked, I did the only thing I could. I set down the boxes and began to pace. I passed makeshift cubicles constructed in the center of the large room. Most cubicles contained older cribs or baby gates, but I passed a few twin beds with lanky teenage limbs spilling over the sides. As I took a few more steps, I saw small rooms flanking the outer edges of the great room. Each had a window where I could look in on the four to five sleeping children in each closet-sized space.

The kids sprawled across toddler beds shoved cockeyed into a space probably meant for a desk or chair. They collapsed on beds in wild sleeping positions, their blankets snarled around their legs. Their hair covered their faces, their small hands in fists against their mouths. They had probably long since outgrown sucking on their fingers, but the comfort may have helped them sleep while removed from home.

I walked from one window to the next, the ladies trying to point out the sibling groups. For an eerie moment, I felt like a shopper in a puppy store, with the sales associate eager to make a commission. Those little puppy children remained curled in those beds, the only movement the flickering of an eyelid possibly visualizing a home where they could be hugged, wanted, and always given priority.

A couple of times, the workers entered the small room and lifted a blanket or hand so that I could see the angelic face underneath. It was like lifting a price tag to advertise a sale. And yet, in my heart, if I could, I would take any one of them home. What were their stories? What had they endured to be left in this cramped puppy-store prison? Did their dreams include lovely escapades, or were they reliving the nightmares that brought them here in the first place?

I covered my mouth and prayed silently. *Father, I have seen Solace in my dreams. She is not here. I thought I would recognize her instantly. I'm not seeing her. What do I do?*

I stalled, reviewed the sibling groups in my mind, and wandered back to the staff for more insight.

They tried to enlighten me with, "Oh yes, the little one who held my hand on the playground—she has a seven-year-old sister at Sunrise Hospital" and "Oh, we don't have any information on those boys. They've only been here since six o'clock last night. The family is all in Texas. Mom is in prison."

I idled, analyzing the sibling-group information sheets. The flash of inspiration never came. If Solace was not here, then there were two reasons: 1) it was not time for her to come to my family or 2) someone else needed me right now. Confusion fogged my mind as the decision loomed.

I retraced my steps, straining to see a difference in the papers. There was a sibling group that consisted of Jaslene and Ramello, ages three and two; Molly and Mikey, both age two; and Jace and

Brock, ages two and one. I wanted to rule out the two boys immediately. Solace was not there. Jaslene looked a little like Solace, though her hair was a much lighter brown. I could not see her eyes as she was still asleep. I couldn't help but wonder if they were blue.

As I shakily gripped the papers, thumbing for insignificant but significant details, the rat-eyed woman came and snatched the papers from my hands. "These two are no longer available," she said. "Another family will be taking them home." She turned on her heel and opened the door, plunking the paperwork on a desk in the lobby. She sprinted back, eyeing the remaining papers in my hands.

*Interesting*, I thought to myself. *Just when I was leaning in that direction.* So, the remaining choices were Molly and Mikey, two redheaded, green-eyed kiddos, or Jace and Brock, two very likely adoptable boys.

"What do you know about these kids?" I asked, pointing to the boy and girl.

The flushed woman shuffled her feet, her scuffed canvas shoes worn into the curves of her feet by hours of running for health information sheets and warning visitors about confidentiality. She cleared her throat and admitted, "Not much. We do know that, originally, they were taken from their home for a few different reasons. They lived in horrendous conditions under blankets stretched behind an abandoned shed. They tried to make rooms outside to, you know, make the best of their condition."

Dinah added, "You should also know that both kids had such horrible cases of lice that their heads were shaved." I flinched at the mention of the little bugs. My heart ached for the little ones scrunched under a torn quilt flapping with each dry gust of desert wind.

"The children have been treated and have been doing well with the 'cottage routine' here, but you should know that Molly is a little mommy and is on the bossy side," said the rat-eyed woman.

I smiled at the thought. *I would need a fiery little girl if I was going to take her home to the gauntlet of three spirited brothers awaiting her. Four, if Mikey came too. She would need to hold her own.*

I knew I was taking too long to decide. I excused myself to step outside and call Keith.

"It sounds like there is only one choice for us. The two little boys' ages fit better with our family, and they would most likely need a permanent home, but it sounds like Molly and Mikey need someone now," he said as I plugged my opposite ear to block out the sounds of traffic.

As I explained each of the situations to Keith, I felt drawn to Molly and Mikey. "M&M," we would call them. I grinned. *Cute.* I arranged to pick them up the following morning. No need to wake them from their naps and disrupt their lives again without fair warning. Plus, it would give me a few more hours to finish some laundry and prepare for the new little ones.

• — ● — •

I glanced at the wrinkled list I'd tugged from my pocket. I knew what I needed to pick up; I just needed assurance. I wandered into the little girls' section of the store. How many times had I tried to buy something from here only to turn around and walk the other direction? Every spring, Easter dresses with beautiful, delicate swirls called out to me, beckoning me closer only to dash my hopes for a little girl on the rocks of reality. I had avoided those sections. Ignored them. Put blinders on as I walked past.

And now, here I was, wondering about the difference between leggings and stretchy jeans, never thinking it would happen.

Would she be a girly girl and want to twirl in a sparkly ruffled dress until it billowed up around her legs? Would she be an active girl, wearing spandex and T-shirts as she hiked to the top of Red Rock Canyon? Would she like pink? I'd hated pink as a little girl. Purple too. I'd lived through a decade without touching the blasted colors.

I lifted a yellow sundress with a large daisy on the front and a brown belt. I coupled it with some navy leggings, a good medium for a nonpink, nongirly, kinda active type of girl. I rubbed the material to see how soft it was. I checked the elastic on the pants to see if a little one could negotiate them in a potty emergency. I anguished between flip-flops and tennis shoes and decided on neither.

The boys' section was much easier. I knew where to find the clearance shorts, T-shirts, and button-up polo shirts that could be worn to church. I circled the racks quickly, arranging seven masculine but practical outfits in no time flat.

At home, I laid each outfit against the couch, pairing its matching bottoms with it. Tomorrow morning, we would have five children altogether. I refrained from saying their ages out loud. *Thirteen, six, two, two, and two. We weren't just crazy. We teetered at the brink of insanity.*

## Questions for the Reader:

*What skills or talents have you developed over the course of your life? Some come naturally; others take work.*

*How can you share your talents and skills with those around you?*

# The Little Ones

I tucked the business card into my back pocket and sighed, completely clearing away any remaining nerves. I had read in the New Testament that morning, "Whatsoever is right I will give you."[3] Though Jesus Christ had taught this sentiment to His Apostles, I felt it applied to me. If this scenario was not meant to be, someone would pry it from my fingertips to show me a better way. But I felt it. That warm feeling enveloped me, rendering me immune to doubt, discouragement, and the worst-case-scenario thinking patterns that had so often overwhelmed me in the past.

I stepped past the security desk and nestled into a single leather chair. A wooden frame nailed to the wall offered stacks of ragged books with corners bitten off by toddler teeth. When the clicking of heels echoed against the tile and a woman called my name, I gripped my purse tighter and stood to shake her hand.

"Good morning." She nodded, her youthful eyes kind. Even in a tailored suit, she did not look like she could shoulder the role of placement coordinator in a temporary orphanage.

"Are you Sam Tyler?" I ventured.

"I am, Mrs. Barlow. It's a pleasure. Thank you for coming down this morning."

I immediately liked Sam Tyler, though from the name on the business card, I had expected a man. Sam flipped her dark ponytail over her shoulder and led me toward a group of toddlers lined up inside the door. Swimming against the current, Sam moved through the line, motioning me forward. A little redheaded boy stepped forward to reclaim his place in line. "Uh-uh," Sam said. "Molly, today you are coming with me."

It took only seconds for it to register that this was Molly. *My* Molly, not some little boy with a faux-hawk. She met my eyes with a shy, quiet glance, her bright-green eyes contemplating me, her lids lowered slightly but evaluating. She wore a plain lavender T-shirt, something I would later learn she would never have chosen. She wore a set of too-small white skater shoes with a fat-lip tongue and unicorns on the sides. She stood pigeon-toed, asking over and over, "Where's Mikey?"

Sam leaned over and whispered to the woman at the desk. Despite the commotion of snack time, for just a moment, I heard Molly hum the tune of the Baby Shark song. I knelt down, locked my hopeful eyes on the confident little girl, and began to sing along with her. Her green eyes crinkled at the edges, and her hands flew to her mouth, partially hiding the wide grin on her face.

"Do you know that song, Molly?" I asked.

The little girl's chin bobbed up and down as a stout little boy appeared at her side. He wore an orange-and-blue-striped T-shirt with a pair of gym shorts that hung almost to his sock line. His shaved head glistened with stubs of strawberry-blond hair. His basset-hound eyes stared up at me, his hands at his side. Molly hugged him close to her. He let her.

I climbed into the back seat, shuffling little bodies into car seats and fumbling with the five-point buckle system. The kids, expressionless, observed me closely as I dug under their legs for the buckles. I perspired, unsure if the midday sun had warmed my car enough to make it uncomfortable or if it was the DFS worker standing outside my car, watching my every move. The kids waved goodbye and submitted to driving away without a word.

I stopped at the light and turned around to look at them. "Do you guys like dogs? I have a dog at my house. Her name is Brinley. She likes kids. She might even try to give you a kiss."

"You have a dog?" Molly asked. She spoke for both of them, an authoritative gesture of not backing down.

"Yeah, a puppy. She's just a little dog. But I bet if you throw a ball for her, she'll catch it and run back with it. She likes that game."

"What about Mikey? Can Mikey play with her?"

"Sure. Can he throw a ball?" I asked.

"But what if she bites Mikey? He will have blood dripping down his arm. What if she eats his hand?"

"I'm not worried about that. She's a nice dog." I glanced in the mirror, trying to read their expressions. Worried that I might have tapped into a traumatic event already, I changed the subject.

"Molly, do you guys like going to parks? We have a big one right by our house."

"A park?"

"Yeah, we can walk there. There are slides, swings, and lots of friends to play with."

"Hmmm."

"If you want, we can go to the really big park too. That one has a big pond with ducks. Sometimes we bring pieces of bread to feed the ducks."

"Will a duck eat Mikey's hand? What if he gets too close?"

"I don't think ducks have teeth to eat Mikey's hand."

"Yes, they do. They will bite his fingers and his arms, and blood will gush out like a Chuckie."

"What's a Chuckie?"

"A bad guy."

This was not going well. I tried another tactic. "Look at those statues! They look like horses to me. Do they look like horses to you? What are they doing in the middle of the road?"

"They are going to get hit by a car and be killed."

Silence. Maybe silence was better. That was enough conversation. I guided the car to the freeway entrance, grateful to have the hum of the tires to block out the awkward conversation. I merged into the flow of traffic.

"We're going to get into a crash. A car will hit us, and we're all going to die," the cartoon voice continued.

"No, I'm a good driver. We're just driving home. I won't let a car hit us. We're not going to die."

I drove on, tallying all these comments in my head. I had yet to hear from Mikey. If I did, would his words take the same graphic turn as Molly's?

"What's your name?" Molly pressed.

"Remember? Chani. You can call me Chani."

"Yeah, I'm not calling you that. My mom will be mad."

"That's okay, what do you want to call me?"

She ignored me and repeated, "My mom will be so mad."

I let it be.

"Look, Mikey! A big truck down there." Molly pointed toward the median where they were constructing the new bridge for the freeway.

I perked up and answered, "That's where they're building the new road. Pretty soon this will all be one big road."

"What if we fall down there?"

"We won't fall. We're not even close to it."

"We will fall, and then we will die."

*Oh, my goodness!* I thought. *What child have I brought home?*

We pulled into the garage and shut the door behind us, and Huddy came running out to meet us. His bare feet whished against the garage floor as he skipped up to the car. His two-year-old smile could warm any heart, and I was proud he was so excited to meet our newest family members. The M&Ms clutched their nearly empty bags and wrapped their arms around their bodies.

The rest of the family joined us in the garage. I introduced everybody one by one.

No response.

I hovered close as Brinley wagged her tail and sniffed their shoes.

I had stayed up late the night before and hung all their clothes in the closet, tags still dangling from the sleeves. The very first hint of excitement crept into Molly's voice when she saw the clothes. She dropped her hands and reached for the pink dress with the flowy skirt. "Is this mine?"

"Of course it is. Do you want to see it?"

The little girl pulled on the hem until the dress popped off the hanger. She stripped off her shirt and leggings in the closet and yanked the itchy tag off, tossing it to the floor. She thrust her arms into the sleeves and twirled with satisfaction. She spotted some flower-printed leggings and grabbed them too. Next, three pairs of socks. And a jacket. She wore everything she found. Her body, now padded with layers of clothes, shook with palpable joy.

Mikey discovered a gym bag in a corner with a basketball hidden inside. He gripped it in his pudgy hand and chucked it across the room, then pointed at it and looked at me expectantly. I gave it back. The process repeated. His hangdog expression lightened, a toothless grin appearing each time the ball bounced. He plowed through the piles of clothes yanked off their hangers and tripped over his own feet. I gasped as he slammed onto the floor, an unexpected, baritone giggle finally emerging.

With all the little ones corralled in the hallway, we knelt down together. I explained that at the end of the day, our family said a prayer before bedtime. The M&Ms stared blankly at us while

Cade thanked God for a nice day, for Star Wars, and for the new kids in our family.

The following day at church, Molly leaned over to Mikey and whispered, "He's here! We're going to meet him!" She sat on her wiggly fingers and rocked forward, too excited to keep still.

"Who are you going to meet?" I asked, confused.

"Jesus! We talked to Him last night, remember? He's here! You said that church is His house!"

I tried to explain that Jesus didn't literally live in the building, but they narrowed their eyes and shook their heads. I struggled to keep up with them as they sprinted down the halls, bumping into the knees of oncoming hallway traffic. They peeked around every corner and in every bathroom stall, fully expecting to meet the man from their prayers.

## Questions for the Reader:

*At the end of the day, it's easy to catalog what didn't get done on the to-do list. How can you give yourself credit for what you accomplish each day?*

*Are you doing your best? That's all God asks of us.*

# Some Doubts

Mikey could talk, but only in the form of four-letter cuss words. He weaved F-bombs expertly through his vocabulary as nouns, adverbs, adjectives, and verbs—a painter with only a couple of brushstrokes. A scowl and middle finger usually accompanied his words. His eyes darkened, and his jaw jutted out against his toothless frown. I often wondered exactly how he'd knocked out his front teeth.

He was a big kid, tall, with a rotund belly and chubby fingers that savagely ripped bananas out of my hands by the bunch. He shoveled food into his mouth from whatever plate he could find on the table and stored it in his cheeks for later. While he used his impressive stature to bully his way to the soccer ball in the toy bucket, he constantly fell off chairs and barstools, tripping over his puffy light-up shoes. He epitomized "bull in a china shop."

Mikey possessed three facial expressions: the "I hate your guts" scowl, a surprised O on his lips when I started to fill the bathtub for the first time, and his sad, Bassett-hound look when I left the room after reading stories. He turned to sassy Molly for protection, for guidance, for an example. He revolved around her, waiting for her orders. She manipulated grand schemes; he cleared a path for her.

Molly wished for a daily fashion show of ruffly, sequined ballgowns but settled for her most colorful Sunday dresses. As a backup, she chose her princess swimsuit and shiny black Mary Janes. I tried to slick down her jagged red mohawk, but a pair of novice clippers had hacked it so unevenly it stood involuntarily. Without parental permission, I couldn't even it out or soften it into something more feminine. She despised being mistaken for a boy and compensated by wearing as many necklaces as possible.

I saw a deeply troubled teenager in her, one whose innocent eyes had seen horrible scenes of violent knife attacks, abuse, and severed limbs. She related it all matter-of-factly, without fear or shock. As I reeled from her stories and took copious notes, those eyes calculated how to get the chocolate chip cookies from the top shelf. At almost three years old, she had lived as an independent adult, and she expected us to treat her like one. In glimpses, I thought I saw the heart and soul of a young child yearning to be free from such heavy responsibility. But when she cannonballed into the pool for the first time or I walked her out on a paddleboard on the lake, I didn't have to dig too deep. The innocent, fun-loving, two-year-old self still thrived, even under all her protective layers.

• — ● — •

I sorted the soiled clothes into towering piles threatening to topple as the M&Ms stomped through each one. They tried to catch the clothes as I tossed them from pile to pile, then let the shirts cover and bury them when they got tired of trying to catch the clothes.

"Why are you washing my stars shirt?" Molly asked.

"You already wore it, baby girl. It's dirty. We're going to wash it so that you can wear it again."

"But I didn't pee on it."

"I know, but after we're done wearing clothes, we wash them."

"But I promise I didn't pee on it."

"I know. It's something different here. We wash our clothes pretty often. Do you want to help me pull the clothes out of the dryer?"

The two toddlers shoved and scrambled to grab the pink square basket. The dryer door flung open, ricocheting off the wall. Clean clothes flew out of the tumbler, propelled by excited little hands, now mixing clean clothes with dirty. Molly grabbed a heated pair of pajama bottoms and buried her face in them. Her eyes closed, relishing the scent, the feel, the warmth of it all. One by one, she grabbed pieces of laundry, holding them up to her nose. "Ahhh," she whispered.

"Okay, who wants to push the buttons on the washer?"

"I do! I do!" They used their bare feet to scale the sides of the baskets.

I lifted each child to push a button and then lifted them again so they could see the water pouring into the basin. The clothes began to spin. They squealed as they, too, began to spin in circles, bumping into the shelves in the laundry room and knocking over the garbage can. Then, when the noise got too loud, they ducked into the hallway, thrilled and terrified by this newfound experience of a washing machine.

• — ● — •

I had fallen into a well-deserved slumber, wet hair matted against my freshly washed pillowcase, pillow tucked under my arm, when I heard a muffled whimper from the depths of the hallway—not a cry, not tears, but a slow, mournful wail surely stifled by snotty hands and trembling little shoulders. I walked toward the noise. In the middle of the hallway, a small figure in pink ballerina jammies huddled even smaller. The whimpering continued, and I approached carefully.

"Molly, what's the matter?"

The little girl turned her blotchy red face toward me, a stream of saliva extending from her mouth to her chest. She remained crouched, covering herself with her hands. As I reached out to touch her, she recoiled.

"Molly, it's okay. You can tell me."

She shifted her hands, revealing a wet backside. The insides of her legs were drenched, and the overpowering smell of urine engulfed the small space. The pee had dribbled from her room to this spot, where it bloomed into one big circle around her.

"Oh no. It's okay. Accidents happen. Here. Let's get you cleaned up."

The little girl flung her body against the wall, refusing to remove her clothes. After some coaxing, she took a few small steps toward the bathroom door. She accepted a wet rag and soap and cleaned up her legs. I offered her a pair of dry jammies, and the whimpering calmed into a soft sniffle, her shoulders occasionally shuddering as her breathing evened out.

I took her back to her bed and rubbed her back until she finally drifted off, hidden well beneath the blanket. Long after she fell asleep, I pictured what life must have been like for a little one to be so afraid of having an accident when her body couldn't hold it any longer.

• — ● — •

The very first night with the kids, I happened to grab *Brunhilda's Backwards Day*, a vividly colored picture book. I sat in the hallway with all four little ones, on neutral ground. The M&Ms fidgeted, unaware of the power within the pages, as I voiced *Brunhilda* with a falsetto, nasal cackle. With a flourish and an invisible twinkle, my fingers cast magic spells. "Poof!" I cried out, turning the page. Entranced, the kids' mouths opened, their jammies stuck against the wall. Eager fingers grabbed at the shiny pages, tearing at them to see what happened next. When I finished, they clapped their hands on the tops of their legs. "Again!" they shouted. We read *Brunhilda* every night they slept in my home.

Tonight was typical of the routine. I closed the book and set it on the floor, and Molly carried it to her room, where she placed it under her pillow. Mikey stepped forward, ready for his nightly jet pack. His large belly jiggled as we pretended to strap the blasters to his shoulders. We pushed a few buttons and counted down: "Five, four, three, two, one . . . Blast off!" We flew him around the room, his giggle tumbling out of his mouth as we plunked him in bed for a safe landing.

Molly preferred a more subtle approach. She reached out her hands for a hug, but I cautioned, "Okay, but no snoring."

She nodded, smirking.

As I reached in for a hug, a snort sounded in my ear. She squealed and grinned so wide I could see all her baby teeth at once. Her little nose crinkled, and her hands flew to her face. She reached out a few more times, snorting in my ear each time. When she finally said her "for reals" good night, she wrapped her arms tightly around my neck and whispered, "Stay, Chani. Please stay."

## Questions for the Reader:

*What can you do to better see the goodness in those around you?*

*What steps can you take toward forgiveness and mending relationships?*

# What's Best

The toy room quickly emerged as a landlocked territory decimated hourly by scattered Hot Wheels and Legos. Today, two-year-old Hudson stared down his nemesis, two-year-old Mikey. Two alpha toddlers. Never touch Hudson's purple blanket! Of course, whenever Mikey reacted, his slightly older two-year-old defender, Molly, stepped in, hands on her hips. Six-year-old Cade evened out the front lines. I felt awful—and had for a while. But even on a good day I didn't have enough hands to hold back the tide of sweat-lathered foreheads charging toward each other. Before I knew it, Molly had planted a couple of right hooks in Huddy's face.

I proposed a two-minute solo time-out on the chair for Molly. She refused. By default, she chose to do time-out with me, so I braced myself against the cushion, legs slightly apart to avoid the frantic kicking of the shrieking, squirming child in my lap. When she arched her back, tossing her weight toward me and throwing me off-balance, I circled my left arm around her chest. While I could not see her face, I could feel the tremors in her wildcat body, her boiling fury. She leaned down and bit the tender skin on the back of my hand. I let her. I would take a picture of the red, raw crescent and send it to the caseworker.

Spitting out profanity, she flailed and threw her head back into my chest. If she hit my collarbone, she could do some damage. Each time she flung her head back, I shifted slightly so that she hit my shoulder instead. She paused for just a moment, then continued harder and more ferociously.

I counted in her ear, "One, two, three, four, five," and took a deep breath so she could feel the movement of air filling my lungs and my exaggerated breath as I exhaled over her shoulder. Her almost-orange eyebrows creased, and she began to claw at my arms, but I continued counting. "One, two, three, four, five." Deep breath.

While she didn't breathe with me, she began to scream the next numbers. "Four! Five!" The scratching stopped, but my arms stung, and I knew it would leave a mark. Her body heaved as she sank against me, still defiant and kicking occasionally but willing to play my game.

"Are you calm enough to apologize? You cannot punch Huddy. That's one of our family rules. Look at how sad he is."

Her lips pursed, and she shook her head.

"All right, we can sit here for a little longer until you're ready."

She kicked backward and forward, aiming for my shins. The wispy hackles on her neck raised, and her eyes narrowed. At last, she conceded. "Sorry, Huddy," she mumbled through clenched teeth.

"Can you tell Chani sorry too? Look. You made my arms bleed."

"Sorry, Chani." She risked a glance and seemed genuinely surprised by the red marks. "Sorry."

"Thanks, baby." I hugged her and sent her back into the toy room. As she skipped toward the others, I felt a throb in my shoulder. I leaned against the chair and coughed into my arm. I needed to rest, but I knew that within the next fifteen to twenty minutes, someone else would scream or cry and I would need to repeat the whole thing. My training required a calm voice, but my voice wavered, ready to crack. I had hit the wall an hour ago. I pled with the kids. They could avoid all these time-outs if only they resisted the urge to retaliate. No one conceded.

I pressed my head against the throw pillow, its embroidered stripes now frayed and barbed. My head pounded, and I couldn't remember if I ate the toast from this morning. I tried to pinpoint the moment when *the change* hit our family. It might have been at my first meeting with the kids' caseworker, Lydia Horne. The county had finally assigned her to us after over a month of waiting. She sat on my living room couch, her artificially blonde hair pulled back into a severe ponytail. She bobbed her head, wagging that ponytail as I highlighted the kids' growing struggles. By then, I had collected pages of horrific background information and evidence of every kind of abuse imaginable. Since she was M&Ms' legal guardian, I handed it over to her. She did nothing! When all the therapists, counselors, and supervisors forced Lydia to explain her inaction, she retaliated.

A week ago, Craig Village had called to warn us that Lydia had filed a charge against us with Child Protective Services (CPS). The charges had no foundation, but I had woken up, every day for the last week, worried that CPS would show up at my door, unannounced, hear the sheer volume of screams and crashes, and whisk everyone I loved into a county van. I rubbed my temples. My heavy eyelids threatened to close, my body desperate for a breather. But I had no choice. It was only 10:30 in the morning.

Mikey stumbled into the room, rubbing his forehead, a fresh red mark swelling into a lump. I sent Cade into the corner and set the timer on the microwave for six minutes. Molly squawked from the other room. I buckled Huddy in the highchair he had long since outgrown and locked the tray against him, then set the timer on my phone for two minutes.

While I set the timers, Molly snuck into the pantry and emerged with a box of chocolate chip Teddy Grahams. Triumphant, she shoved a fistful in her mouth and gloated at Cade. He screamed and dashed across the room, stealing the box, shaking fragmented crackers all over the floor, which was still wet from the toddlers getting into the fridge just minutes before.

I separated the kids, placing one back in time-out and the other back in the playroom. I took the torn Teddy Grahams box and put it with my cake pans above the fridge. The house was too quiet. I searched for Mikey and found the sliding doors ajar. In the backyard, Mikey rode the Big Wheel over the stone patio with the finesse of an Indy 500 racer, his bare feet his only brakes against the hot stones. He chuckled as he sped through the sandbox spraying the window with his wheels. I could leave him there for a minute.

The timer sounded, a shrill reminder that the others needed me. I practiced my calm voice, and Cade and I discussed why he went into time-out. Sometimes I wondered if I would ever get to use my adult voice again. I was tired of the mommy-is-serious tone. Again, I had a couple of minutes.

*I can't do this. This is ridiculous. My own personal hell.* My chest rattled again, and I stifled another cough before it climbed up my throat. I was sick of being sick. I swiped at a few tears dribbling out the corner of my eyes and knew it would help to talk it out. I took a deep breath.

*Heavenly Father, I don't know how much time I will have to talk to you, and I'm sorry that I'm not even bowing my head. I mean no disrespect, but I hope you can see what is going on.*

*Heavenly Father, I'm not sure what's happening right now. I know it is fruitless to question why we have to experience hard times, but I'm not sure what I need to learn from this situation. My boys are completely unhappy. Huddy hardly talks anymore. He just hides in the corner with his blanket. Cade just screams over anything; I feel like I can never pull down the Lego boxes for his reward. I know Tyson has more freedom to leave than the others, but he's hard to read. I know he's struggling. Father, I am miserable. Keith is suffering. This is not what we expected.*

*You know better than anyone that I was angry about the prospect of adding to our family again. I felt maxed out then. It took awhile to convince me, but I came around. I wanted to make a difference. I knew I couldn't change the system—*

I heard the Big Wheel slam against the sliding door, its wheels crackling over the sand-littered patio. It backed up and rammed it again.

"Mikey, buddy, we don't crash into the walls. Ride around the patio."

*I'm sorry, Father. I guess I expected something different. I knew the foster-care classes tried to prepare us for the worst-case scenario, but this is far beyond anything I thought. I'm exhausted. I'm so tired. I just can't keep up. I know that there are times when you can take the burden away, and I know there are times when you give us the strength to endure. I'm not sure which to pray for right now.*

*But, Father, I am done. I really can't imagine living like this much longer. My cough is still there. It's been over three weeks, and I can't even picture trying to schedule an appointment for myself with the doctor. I'm chained to the house. Going out in public with this crew is way beyond me.*

Huddy's muffled cry caught my attention. I opened the door to the garage to find him with one large baseball cleat on his left foot, his right foot bare. Molly smugly held the other shoe in her hand and was trying to place her flip-flop in it. Huddy threw his head back and wailed.

"Molly, was he wearing those shoes?"

She merely shoved the shoe behind her back. I bent over her and grabbed it from her, then shoved Huddy's dirty foot back into it. He seemed satisfied, and she stomped away, glaring at me, then grabbed the scooter and rode around the empty garage space.

*That's it, Father. I have been powering through for weeks. I can't keep up with all the therapy appointments. Every day is a new problem and something even more serious than the day before. Yesterday, I caught them lying on top of each other, grinding and kissing. That was the last straw. I love those kids, Father, but I can set aside my pride long enough to realize that I can't give them what they need.*

*I'm doing my very best, but now CPS is involved. We documented all the abuse. DFS filed a retaliatory complaint against us, and I'm worried they will knock on my door and take everyone away from me. My best is just not enough. I know I am responsible for my own decisions, and I'm going to contact the agency today. It's time. I'll give them our thirty-day notice to remove the M&Ms. It's not fair to anyone right now.*

My bottom lip quivered, and I pressed the tips of my fingers against it to stifle the shaking. I swiped at my runny nose.

*You are always in my heart, Heavenly Father. I wish I could talk to you even more, but I'm sure you're tired of hearing from me. I feel like I haven't felt you near me in a while. I don't know if you're disappointed with me. Please don't leave me hanging. Not right now. Please let me feel of your peace. Please let me borrow your strength, at least until Keith comes home.*

I pulled out my phone and began to text Keith but quickly shut it off when the two toddlers, now red-faced, began to tussle on the ground, one holding two plastic swords, the other nothing.

I lifted Mikey, a solid forty pounds of sheer destruction, and separated the two.

I called everyone into the living room. Reluctantly, they filed in, some flopping upside down on the couch, others warily trudging in. I faked a bit of optimism with a singsong chant. "Guess what today is! Guess what today is!" I clapped.

They looked up, intrigued.

"Today is Donut Day! Who would like a donut?"

Four hands shot into the air; some bounced a couple of times.

"Okay, here's the plan. We're going to make some turkey sandwiches, and if we stop fighting, I will take you to pick out a donut."

"Yay!" The collective shout raised the roof and thudded against the walls. Molly turned a circle in her Minnie Mouse dress, bumping into Cade. He backhanded her across the face, and she reacted with a punch to the arm.

"Uh-uh. For reals. No fighting, and I mean it. If we fight, we won't get a donut." They slipped away, each to finish their own to-do list, and I pulled out the turkey, mayo, mustard, and bread. I pulled out a knife and the cheese, but before I could slice it, a handful of pebbles hit the sliding glass door. "All right, Mikey, we're done out here if we're going to throw the rocks. You guys know the rules." I couldn't handle the neighbors ringing my doorbell again. I ushered a smiling Mikey back inside to find Molly on the counter, mustard in hand. She'd flung the tamper-proof cap haphazardly across the table, and mustard dripped down Minnie Mouse.

"Can I help?" she asked.

I grabbed a rag, cleaned her up, and made the sandwiches, her dirty fingers applying the cheese slices to each. The kids scrambled to get their favorite plates and cups but ultimately ended up pouting when someone else took their plate or snuck a sip from their cup. I rolled my eyes. A couple of time-outs later, my own sandwich had crusted and dried, my chips stolen, my drink spilled across the table. We had to get out of the house, but they were definitely not getting donuts.

• — • — •

Thankful for a couple of God-given moments of peace, I glanced at the sleeping toddlers in the rearview mirror. Tyson had agreed to come along at the threat of losing video-game privileges for the day. He sat in the passenger seat, staring at his phone, pulling up videos of rockets and duct-tape creations.

I whispered, "When we get home, I'm just going to pull into the garage, stay here, and let them sleep. You're welcome to get out and do whatever you want for the rest of the day."

He nodded gratefully.

I left the garage door open and the engine running as I pulled out my phone.

*To Whom It May Concern:*

*I am writing to you in regards to the Bentley siblings that were placed in our foster home eight weeks ago. I am respectfully providing our 30-day notice and request that the children be found a more suitable placement to accommodate their needs. I do so for the following reasons:*

1. *I have three boys (ages 13, 6, and 2) who have special needs of their own and already require a higher level of care and professional help. I am not able to meet the needs of two additional highly traumatized children who require various mental and social health professionals, occupational and behavioral therapists, and others to address their developmental lags and psychological con-*

cerns. *There just aren't enough hours in the day. I am spread too thin.*

2. *Both children have exhibited aggression and violent tendencies, including hitting, punching, kicking, biting, scratching, pinching, head-butting, severe language, and flailing. Primarily, I am the target, but these behaviors are now directed at my children and dog. My own boys have begun to reciprocate these actions, creating an excessively hostile environment. This occurs both at home and outside the home.*

3. *Both children have displayed highly sexualized behavior with each other, including kissing, touching, lying on top of each other, reenacting sexual activity and "playing boyfriend." This behavior has now been directed toward my children, requiring my constant supervision all hours of the day. Regardless of history, this is completely unacceptable.*

4. *As with any traumatized child, these children do not respond well to discipline. Molly is highly parentified and independent and immediately rejects anyone else trying to assume a parent's role. Both children will run away at any chance and try to sneak out the front door. Both seem oblivious to the dangers of this and will run through parking lots, down the streets, anywhere to avoid being caught. I am currently having to leave my own little ones to chase them down, a possibly unsafe scenario there as well.*

*I recognize the seriousness of this situation and do not take this decision lightly. I care for these children and want the best for them. Unfortunately, I am not able to provide them with everything they need at this time. It would be a disservice to them and their family to try to do so.*

*Please consider their needs carefully and find a placement where they will be able to heal and move forward after such a difficult time in their lives.*

*You are welcome to contact me with any questions or concerns.*

I read it a couple of times, hearing stirring in the car seats behind me. Good enough. I had taken a formal approach and tried my best to give as many details as possible without sounding whiny. I sent the message and turned around as a disgruntled Mikey found that he was still buckled in. The others woke to his grunts, and in minutes, the car filled with protests.

*It's official. Let's see how the caseworkers respond.*

•—●—•

The garage door lifted, the house rumbling. Brinley barked as she pranced down the stairs and hurdled the bench in the entryway. Huddy heard it next, abandoning his blanket and sprinting to greet Daddy. I dove to the back door, pressing it safely shut until I heard the engine stop and the garage door shut behind it, then slid away from my post as a torrent of toddlers rushed over to greet Keith. I heard a collection of honks and locking mechanisms as they scrambled inside and outside the car.

"Hi, Dad!" they shouted, each ready to be lifted in the air, high above the others. He did "rocket ship," counting down to blastoff and jet propelling them each into space. Keith rounded the corner with Molly high in the air, providing convincing explosions and engine-malfunction sound effects. He lifted her high enough to touch the lip of the entryway, the beads around her neck dangling.

He set her down, and she beamed up at him. "You're the best daddy we've ever had," she confessed.

"Aw, thanks, sweetie. And you're the best Good Golly Miss Molly we've ever had." Keith gave her a hug and watched her run out into the backyard to blow bubbles.

I sucked in a gulp of air and turned toward the wall, biting my lip, then leaned against the counter, waiting for the hot dogs to defrost. My reflection in the microwave door showed a lumpy ponytail with flyaways sticking out in all directions.

Keith pulled me close, cradling my head against his chest, my tears silently seeping into his jacket, my shoulders shuddering as I buried my face against him. I had never been so excited to see my husband.

"It's going to be okay, baby, I promise. It can't continue like this," he said as he stroked my hair.

"I know. I sent the email today."

"I saw it. Perfect. And I think we should follow it up with a phone call to DFS saying that we expect our case to be expedited because of the fraud they committed on their end. Any legal timelines are waived at that point."

"No, I just barely sent it. Let them respond before you go bulldog on them."

"But they misled us. They knew about the kids' issues before they were placed with us. Youth Harbor knew! How could they not? The M&Ms weren't part of the nineteen kids removed that night. Youth Harbor had Molly and Mike for two weeks! It only took us a couple of days to see all the red flags."

"Oh, that reminds me, I spoke with the therapist this morning. She mentioned that her supervisor already had a record of their behaviors on file before she reported them herself. Another therapist evaluated the kids on day one. That's not normal. They only do that in extremely rare situations. Miss Sarah said the kids were described as 'feral cats' on the original report. Not to add fuel to the fire, but that's another person who knew."

"And they still went ahead with everything?" Keith said as he clenched his jaw.

I nodded, watching him. I knew he was chewing on a sarcastic response but swallowed it instead. He knew I suffered in the trenches and tried his best to alleviate the pain in our home. Ever the peacemaker, he tried to insulate the battered, hollow version of his spunky wife and protect our family—even if he was a bulldog peacemaker.

"This will be for the best," I added. It hurt to think that the agency had to do a bait and switch to find a home for the M&Ms. I couldn't juggle all their problems, but I dreaded the thought of someone else being duped. I didn't admit it out loud, but I had failed. My worst fear. I didn't want to disappoint anyone, and I felt like I had disappointed everyone. The kids. My family. My husband. God. He'd trusted me to help Him out, and I'd let Him down. It sickened me to picture the kids moving from foster home to foster home.

"Did you see Candace's response to my email?" I asked, sitting down on the bottom stairs, where I could still see the kids outside.

He shook his head. "What did she say?" Keith ignored a foam Nerf bullet whizzing past his ear.

"She says the agency will do anything they can to support us in the next thirty days. She suggested putting the kids in daycare to give us a break during the day."

"Not a bad idea."

"No, but since birth mom is an antivaxxer, I can't." I threw my arms up and smiled with a sarcastic what-else-could-go-wrong eye roll.

"When did you find that out?"

"Yesterday at visitation."

"She refuses to vaccinate her kids?" He raised his eyebrows and picked up Hudson, who clung to his leg like a leech.

"I don't care, but that puts us in a sticky situation. We can't leave them in any public daycare setting."

"Did you tell Candace?"

"She knows. I've filled her in on it, but she must have forgotten. She also says she hopes this hasn't spoiled us on foster care." I grimaced.

"I don't think it has, but I'm going to need a break." He nodded toward the backyard.

"Me too, but I don't even know if that will do it. I'm done."

"We'll see. Let's not even think about it now. What's for dinner?" He called in the troops and set the table.

I sliced the watermelon into triangles, placing them into the plastic bowl. *Nope*, I thought. *We're done.*

## Questions for the Reader:

*I once had a friend tell me that to feel closer to God, he avoided the "three Cs:" contention, conflict, and controversy. What can you do to eliminate these from your home?*

# Now What Do I Do?

Mikey and Molly clutched their Nike duffel bags to their bodies as they stoically climbed into the car seats, refusing to look at me. They didn't want to hug me goodbye. I didn't blame them. Another van ride meant another house, new rules, a lot of adjusting, and fear of the unknown. I waved as the van backed up and signaled to turn onto Rancho Drive. I couldn't see through the dark windows, and I don't know if the M&Ms waved back. Keith and I held each other in the parking lot long after the van drove away.

Who was going to dance around the kitchen with them, hands held high in the air, twirling and singing the peanut-butter-jelly song? Who would read *Brunhilda* and cackle just like me? They could repeat the story by heart. I wasn't concerned about that. I wanted to feel that they needed me. That maybe I had contributed to their lives just a little bit.

For days, I retreated to the library with laptop open, hoping for a quiet place to type out my thoughts, but the words dammed up inside. I slumped against the chair and tried to cough out the stories that had been swirling in my mind for the past few days. Writing had always been therapy for me, and I needed it. I needed it badly. After our storm had passed, leaving a path of destruction, I wandered through the sparkly things, the beautiful times, the good moments.

I remembered mixing brownies and the screech of the barstool dragged across the tile floor. Stepping aside as the chair was shoved in my way no matter where I placed my bowl. Little hands climbing up to the countertop, leaving a trail of ingredients in their wake. The flour jar, open. The bag of walnuts, emptied. The can of cocoa wafting into the kitchen sink. Trying to stir the dusty components before they splattered across the room when Molly took over. Pouring the batter into the pan, then offering a drippy beater to the girl.

"Take this. Lick it," I encouraged.

"Lick it?" Those bright-green eyes formed a line in the middle of her forehead.

"Just hold out your tongue."

A tentative little pink tongue emerged, and she brushed the beater against it.

"Mmmm . . . that's *not* bad," she pronounced and eagerly took the silver utensil in hand, smearing brownie batter all across her face. She parked her barstool in front of the oven door and pressed the palms of her hands and her nose against it. She ignored the heat, her face illuminated by the eerie light panel inside. She didn't want to miss the magic happening inside.

I thought of Mikey peeling out of the driveway, bare toes curled just enough to touch the pedals on the upright bike. He had wheelied onto curbs, releasing belly laughs and singing one line from "Old Town Road" until we couldn't stand it. On swim days, his shirt barely stretched across his middle as he flopped into the pool, his eyebrows arched to his hairline, his smile so wide he burped out water after each dive. Then, he'd cocoon himself in a beach towel, both hands bulging with fruit snacks, the hammock swallowing him alive.

I shook my head, a little misty at the memory, and examined my bare, unpainted fingernails. I missed seeing smears of horrendous purple across my nails, cuticles, and the tips of my fingers. Molly used to raise her confident chin, brush in hand, as she inspected her work. "You need some more on this one," she'd cluck, her pinky held daintily in the air. I tried to ignore the glittery streak oozing down the front of her pants and the blotches of neon pink just outside the towels I'd laid on the floor.

When Molly asked if she could brush my hair, I nodded, handed her the brush, and tilted my head back. She wove her fingers from my scalp to the ends of my hair, reverently brushing the tresses to a shine. She touched her own pixie cut, with its awkward scissor lines in her bangs and above her ears. I could see the hope in her eyes that she would one day have long hair to brush and style.

I sighed, looked around the lobby of the library, pulled up my social media account, and wrote:

*I wish I could detach myself from my surroundings, avoid my feelings by using flowery words and intricate imagery. I could. But the truth is, I'm pretty fragile right now. Powerful words stem from powerful feelings. Right now, I'm a confused, emotional storm. Instead, I'll be real:*

*My two little foster children have moved on to the next chapter of their story. I gave my all. I really did. I traded my health, my hobbies, my peace for three months of the hardest, most intense challenges our family has ever faced. Our house was a war zone, and we are still tending to wounds and counting casualties.*

*That said, I still lie in bed as the sun comes up, tuning my ears to hear the quiet crush of carpet from little feet. They pause in front of my bed and wait patiently for me to open my eyes. A smile spreads as they jump onto my bed, hugging me fiercely and telling me that I am "the best mom they have ever had." All was silent this morning, and it hurts so deep inside that I can't breathe.*

*Did I add to their pain? Did I fail? Did I spread myself too thin? Will they even remember me years from now? I don't know if I will ever know. I'm ashamed to admit my relief, but I'm struggling to let them go. In the Bible, the Savior promises peace. I pray for that. I pray that someday I'll look back on this time with clarity and understanding. For now, if my eyes are a little red or watery today, let's just both agree that there must be a lot of pollen in the air.*

I pushed the Save button and blinked back the tears freely falling down my cheeks. *Why did I write that? I am so private. Now everyone will know. Superwoman has lost her cape, her weaknesses outweighing her strengths.* I swiped at my wet face.

I shut my laptop, unable to truly capture what was on my mind. How did you write how relieved you were to see them go? How you counted down the days? How YOU were the one who'd tossed the white flag into the air? The caseworkers pointed their fingers at you, accusing you of being selfish and not doing your best for the children. You were at fault for their behaviors, their reactions. You added to their trauma—another item for the therapist to address.

The accusations clobbered my thoughts, and I retreated, bruised and battered, into a dark corner of my mind. They weren't true. Logically, I knew it. But I felt the blunt force of each one in my gut. *Failure. Disappointment. Unworthiness.*

I walked out of the glass doors of the library, my favorite T-shirt a little too tight around my middle. What was the point of this fruitless search for Solace? Was this torture? Punishment? I struggled to punch my keys into the ignition, dropping them onto the floor in the sweltering heat. I growled at my clumsiness and thumped the steering wheel. *What was wrong with me?*

I didn't have to look far. Deep in my heart, I knew what was off. It had been months since I felt any connection to heaven. Not that I hadn't tried. I had prayed every day, more fervently than ever. I had poured out my soul to my Savior and felt completely ignored. On hold with an automated response. He was busy.

Once, I tried to describe the silence to Keith. Even to my own ears, it sounded dumb. "It's like I've fallen into a deep pit and can't get out. The walls are closing in, and I need someone to help me. A ladder, a hand up, a rope, anything. But I am so far down and so in the dark that nobody hears me or bothers to reach down."

He nodded, his eyes searching mine for meaning, pitying me and my irrational emotions. He didn't understand. How could he? I know he tried.

I often wondered about that darkness and what it meant. Did the lack of an answer to my prayers mean I was not worthy of His attention? In the scriptures, God ignored groups of people when they ignored Him. He was slow to answer their cries. He did answer but in His own time. I wasn't sure if I had done something to offend God. Was He tired of hearing from me? Had I missed a subtle answer as I'd wailed in my closet, pounding my fists against the carpet, my forehead to the floor?" "*Heavenly Father, where are you? Where are you? You promised you would be here, and you're not! I'm drowning here, and you don't even care. Where are you?*"

Still, the silence lingered. I didn't know how to interpret it. I had done everything I had been asked to do. We'd chased the girl in the dream when it wasn't logical. We'd sold our house in a horrible real estate market, moving away from a comfortable home and a neighborhood we loved. We'd attended months of classes for licensing and submitted to screenings by multiple government agencies who'd finally declared us fit enough to be foster parents.

Did I want to do all those things? Probably not. It would have been easier to finally put the bookend up against our youngest child and call our family complete. As Hudson traipsed off to school, I could look into a position where I could better contribute my talents.

My questions attacked me, one more savage than the next. I felt each doubt rip through the seams of my confidence in my Heavenly Father. *Did God really speak to me years ago? Did I imagine it? Did Keith and I talk about it so much we created our own wishful reality? A placebo effect? It could have been what I ate that night. Maybe a lack of sleep and a hallucination.* I couldn't answer. Nobody could answer me. I hung my head in my hands, smoothing my fingers over my hair over and over. I rubbed between my eyes.

Resigned, I started the car, shoulders slumping a little, hands hanging down. *Oh, I feel so low. So forgotten. I have always seen God in the details of my life, and, now, when I need Him most, He ignores me.* A dull nothingness filled my body. A numbness to counteract the sadness. I didn't smile as I drove home. I didn't cry. I didn't pound the steering wheel. I didn't summon memories, good or bad. I did not wish to end my life, but I didn't know how to move it forward. Which direction was forward anyway?

Nothing mattered. Why try? I placed my purse up on the shelf in the entryway and climbed the stairs, my staring eyes seeing nothing, my exhausted body feeling nothing.

## Questions for the Reader:

*Have you ever felt like God has forgotten you? How did you react?*

*What can you be grateful for today?*

# Baby Girl

I wish I could tell you the call came the next morning—that magical, life-changing call that repeated itself in family folklore for generations, the kind of call that sent you scrambling to the nearest store, throwing everything on the shelf into your basket, the kind of call that made you overlook the fact that you were wearing two different running shoes.

The truth is the phone didn't ring. I'd hoped for it. I'd tried to force it by playing Michael Buble's "Haven't Met You Yet" over and over until my boys kicked the backs of the car seats. The children's hospital had changed marketing tactics and removed its billboard. No long-lost siblings tracked us down, Wisemen-like, bearing gifts, humbly asking us to be their forever family. I often wondered how our story would end. It began with such a miraculous start. I could only imagine how amazing the grand finale would be.

I couldn't control everything around me, but I needed better control over what I could. I dialed a number that had been tucked behind the FAMILY sign on our kitchen counter, a leftover number from the names and resources I had gathered months before. Finally, a mental health counselor. Even as I dialed, I felt deflated, ashamed I had stooped to this point. I penciled in an appointment on my calendar, then a dozen more.

I knew I needed time to heal, to be whole again. I started where I could. I woke up, splashed water on my face, put my two puffy feet on the floor, got dressed, then went for a walk through the neighborhood. My only adult interaction in months began with a wave at the old man in the Gilligan hat and jammies sauntering down the park trail, hands clasped behind his back.

As the days passed, I stopped contemplating the pinecones on the ground ahead of me. I lifted my head and nodded to Delilah, then reached down to pet her pink-eared dog, Bitsy. I introduced myself to Ronald as he helped his wife, Ellen, out of their car. Bundled in a scarf and coat no matter the month, she waved and rolled her walker to the tennis courts. Bonnie dragged her oxygen tank beside her and sat under the pavilion, offering me green apples or string cheese out of the box in her trunk. Cliff, the large man in the red hoodie, gave me a thumbs up every time I passed him. I looked forward to it. I watched for them. I waved at them. They grew important to me.

The first time I met Ray, I passed her on the path by the soccer field, dodging the piles of fallen pine needles that made the path slick and hard to navigate. She walked slowly, her white hair cut tightly against her freckled, light-brown skin. I could see her lips moving, but with my earbuds in, I couldn't decipher what she was saying. I slowed to a walk and yanked the cord out of my ear.

"You know what Mo told me this morning?" she asked.

I shrugged and peeked over my shoulder, not sure who Mo was.

"Mo told me that when he dies and comes back, he wants to be a man. A strong man. He wants all the beautiful ladies to come to him. Isn't that right, Mo?" She bent down with some difficulty and scratched the ears of the gray-and-white terrier staring up at her. She pulled a treat out of the pouch at her waist and stood back, taking me in.

*She thinks her dog talks to her?* I managed a small smile and knelt for Mo to sniff me. His tail wagged.

"I knew it. I knew he'd like you. He likes all the beautiful women here." She edged past me, her flowered leggings shuffling along under her oversized turquoise T-shirt. Mo walked contentedly next to her without a leash. When I put my earbud back in, I could still hear something about pleasing beautiful women. I chuckled as Kelly Clarkson and I rounded another corner.

Each day I saw the woman and Mo, she smiled and looked directly into my eyes. "Good morning!" she always said brightly.

"Morning," I mumbled and jogged away.

After a few weeks of the same exchange, I finally stopped, unashamed of the sweat rolling down my head. "I know I see you every morning, but I don't know your name. I'm sorry. I'm Chani." I reached a hand to her. She took it, not flinching at my sweaty palm.

"It's Raylene. Just call me Ray, or you can just say, 'Hey, baby,' and I'll know you're talking to me."

I laughed out loud and nodded. "Okay, nice to meet you, Ray. Have a good one." I still had two laps before I called it a day.

• — ● — •

The first time I sat on the sofa across from Sam, my therapist, I told him everything—EV-ER-Y-THING—from my childhood trauma to my present foster drama. At that point, I had nothing to lose, no pride to protect, no CPS cases hanging over my head. In my mind, this was my last resort, my only hope before I packed my bags for a permanent stay at a crisis hospital. All I could think of was how pitiful I must seem to him. With every sentence, I tripped over apologies for him having to waste his time on someone like me.

He slowly shook his head and leaned back in his chair, then set his pen and clipboard down on the table beside him. He waited for me to grab another tissue. And then he said it. "Chani, do you want to know what I really think?"

"I dunno. Do I?

He waited for me to meet his gaze. "I'm amazed you're still standing. I can't even imagine the weight of the burden you've carried for so long."

"Really?"

"You are, by far, one of the strongest women I have ever met. Really."

I'd like to say that I gracefully accepted his take on my life, but I wasn't quite ready for it. I ugly cried instead.

It wasn't just because he'd told me I was strong or even validated my pain. Here was one of only a handful of people who knew about the rough patches in my family and the PTSD I'd suffered from my car accident. He didn't tally my mounting imperfections and failures as an adult. He didn't gasp when I questioned my faith and God. I felt liberated. For once, I dropped the facade. I didn't have my crap together. Clumps of my hair and eyelashes had fallen out because of the intense stress. Most days, I barely hung on until it was time to sleep, if sleep came at all.

Sam didn't have a magic concoction for me. In fact, he stepped aside to let me see the logic for myself. He offered neutrality, a voice of reason, to counteract the toxic lies of my inner critic. I'm not going to sugarcoat this. It was hard. My demons were no joke. But trust blossomed, and I learned how to recognize my triggers. I no longer turned to Oreos every time I felt uncomfortable with my emotions. I don't even like Oreos.

When my leg broke, I'd needed (painful!) x-rays and Dr. Harris's surgical tools to repair it. When baby Tyson's stomach had refused to digest his food, he needed to be rushed to the children's hospital for immediate repair. When the physical imbalances in my body created a rush of depression, anxiety, and stress, I sat on Sam's couch, tissues handy. He offered me options: medication, tapping therapy, subtle suggestions, and a listening ear. Though talking about my memories made my throat seize up and swallowing difficult, I always felt better afterward.

If I had known the freedom I would gain from trusting myself to a mental health professional, I would have done it years ago. I recommend it to everyone.

• — ● — •

My house seemed uncharacteristically quiet, and I relished the reprieve from the echo of warring toddlers. To fill the silence, I blasted music every morning, anything I could sing off-key to. I lip-synced *We Are the Champions* into the rearview mirror, causing Hudson to belly laugh. Tyson faked an eye roll when I danced a sassy jive to Ray Charles on "Doo Wop Saturdays." I flung open the windows and talked over my fence with the neighbor's kids about their new puppy.

Each night, I escaped into books. I'd tell myself, "Only one more chapter," and turn page after page, buried in a tense menagerie of whodunnits. I couldn't help it. I'd even skip a sentence or two to reach the climactic ending scenes. I'd mark the page and fall into a restful sleep in the arms of a man who loved me so much I felt unworthy of the love-song lyrics he texted me every day.

On hot summer mornings, I filled the cheap blue plastic pool in the backyard and let the boys squirt me with their water guns. We bombarded the park, overtaking the spaceship from the masses of children clinging to the bars with an arm or a leg. My littles grabbed my pinky and led me to the swings, where I pushed so long I had to alternate arms when my shoulder ached. But I didn't complain. I chucked balled-up socks at my boys in sock wars that left them taking cover behind couches and frantically hurling ammo in my direction. I faked a dramatic death on the living room ottoman only to be dragged onto the floor by a ninja pirate wearing Mr. Potato Head sunglasses and shoes on the wrong feet.

In the mornings, when the house was still, I knelt next to my bed and thanked my Heavenly Father for the rays of light gradually illuminating my life. Though heaven hadn't responded yet, it didn't feel as distant. I figured that at some point, God would answer me. I knew He existed, and I leaned on that knowledge. I wondered if there might be a specific reason for the silence. Was God trusting me to figure this out for myself?

One morning, I happened to read the parable of the Good Samaritan in the New Testament. The Samaritan took compassion on a traveler who had been beaten and abandoned. He cleaned him up and took him to an inn, where he cared for him. The next day, he paid the innkeeper to watch over the traveler. I knew the story well. But I had overlooked one little detail—an aspect I absolutely needed to understand. The Samaritan left. He couldn't stay.

I reread the verses, my eyes misting so that I couldn't see the words on the page. I gulped against the tightening in my throat. I flattened the page and propped my chin on my fist.

The Samaritan had done what he could to make a difference *in the moment.* He hadn't failed. He didn't have to be the primary caregiver from start to finish. Maybe that's how it was with Mikey and Molly. I hadn't failed. Our family was never meant to be their primary caregivers. Our role had been to take them to a certain place on their journey. We'd cleaned them up. We'd shown them love for maybe the first time they had ever been shown love.

We'd identified the abuse, the triggers, and the resources the kids needed. DFS wanted to send them back to Youth Harbor, but we'd handpicked and met with a new foster family who was in a better position to care for their hurts. We hadn't taken the easy route. We hadn't ignored the kids. I sighed, grabbed my pen, and let the realization solidify in ink on the journal page, the weight on my heart lifting with each sentence.

I decided to capture even more of my experiences to make sense of them and provide an outlet for my confusion. I made lists. I tapped my lips with my pen and thought out loud. Most people feel a need to create, to compose music, to decompress in front of an easel with sloppy tubes of watercolor. I wrote.

I took my idea for a book and sat down on the floor of my bedroom, laptop on my legs, a pile of empty Starburst wrappers growing beside me. I wrote about making brownies, smiling as the memories of fake snores and invisible jet packs swirled inside me. I lashed at the keyboard, reliving my time-out failures. It wasn't pretty. I hoped the words flowing from my body would ease the tension in my shoulders and neck. Keith took the boys to the splash pad with the promise of milkshakes just to give me time to myself. Brinley stood sentinel against the locked door, my personal gargoyle.

I stared at the computer screen, trying to find the words to describe the powerful surge I felt in my heart when I thought about that hospital room years ago. The first time I knew God was aware of me. The first time I felt His love for me. I traced that pattern of love to the coincidences in my boys' adoptions and how things "just fell into place." I sighed when I pictured my little Solace. The moment in my memory seemed hazy, slippery even. But I knew her face. My throat throbbed whenever I thought of the billboard and stopping the car just to look at her eyes.

Slowly, imperceptibly, rays of sunshine peeked over the horizon of my mind, and the cold, menacing clouds of discouragement dissipated. I lifted my chin, wondering how long the sun had been up. I wasn't sure when it happened, but it did. As I threw those sock balls, pushed those swings, typed with my back against the corner wall of my bedroom, remembering God's mercies, I found my solace. I couldn't pinpoint the dramatic moment I felt whole again, but I felt it. I knew because I used to avoid the spare bedroom knowing I longed to see a little dark-haired girl asleep in that bed. Now, I could vacuum it without stopping to sit on the edge of the bed and finger the small plastic teacup left behind.

I can't explain it even now. I had felt lost and forgotten, groveling in a dark place. I mentally retraced my steps. There was no secret sauce. I simply put one foot in front of the other. I focused on one doable task at a time. I took deep breaths, not allowing the corrosive accusations of epic failure to creep into my mind. I did my best. More than that, I gave my all. I turned to God even when He seemed to have turned away from me. I could feel glimmers of His peace again, knowing that my faith had been strong enough to withstand His absence.

One Friday evening, I attended a church activity where the speaker set his prepared sermon on the corner of the pulpit. He confessed he had prepared something completely different, but after the opening prayer, he knew he needed to say something specific. *I knew he would do that.* My breathing stopped. Though time didn't pause dramatically, I felt something prick at my heart. *He's about to say something meant for me.* I don't know how I knew it. I spun my wedding ring backward and forward. I wiggled it up against my knuckle and back down again. I couldn't bring myself to make eye contact with him.

The speaker looked directly across the room, over crowds of adults fanning themselves in the desert heat, and pronounced emphatically, "God LOVES broken things. He gives them a chance to mend. He restores them. He makes them better, stronger. He wants us to see the care He takes with broken things. He wants us to trust Him with our brokenness."

I flushed, feeling like the only broken person in the room. *But is that why God put me through all of this? Did He break me? If He wants us to come to Him with our brokenness, why doesn't He answer me?* This time, my questions didn't throb with fiery resentment. I sincerely wanted to know. And just like I knew the message over the pulpit had my name on it, I knew God was ready to answer. I sat taller in my chair and reached for Keith's hand, pulling it onto my lap.

*God didn't break you*, I told myself resolutely. *That's not His nature.* I looked down at Keith's fingers intertwined with mine. *The God I know is a God who loves His children.*

The speaker wasn't done. He pounded the pulpit and leaned into the microphone, letting the volume of his voice echo through the quiet. "Trust that God knows the plan that will best bless His children. Don't flee from the chance to serve Him. What we once thought we couldn't do, we do. And we do it in the sacrifices we are asked to make, things that are personal to us, things that are meaningful to us. God is aware of us." He emphasized each of the last words, his fingers pointing out each syllable. "He knows you. He LOVES you. Oh, if you only knew just how much He loves you."

The floodgates opened. Finally. I felt it inside, the unhindered warmth I'd missed so badly for so long. That unquestionable peace, that divine love, poured into my body, overflowing out of the corners of my eyes. I dug for a tissue, dabbing at my eyes, my nose, my smeared makeup, and the drops falling freely on my shirt. I pinched a second tissue out of the package. Then a third.

*God has always been aware of me. He knows how broken and forgotten I've felt. Just like I know what difficulties my boys have just endured. God saw it all. From day one.* He suffered when my aching body yearned for a few hours of precious sleep and insomnia denied it. He watched me clear my throat to quell the tears when I drove the M&Ms to play "ice cream parlor" and blow bubbles with their new foster mom. He knew about the dirty fingerprints dotting the walls, the torn pages in my favorite book, and Molly's prized little penguin now perched on my laundry room shelf to remind me of her.

*He was there with me. And He is proud of me.*

·—●—·

"Baby Girl!"

I grinned when I saw Ray's outline against in front of the gate of the dog park in the early morning sunlight. Ray's walking buddy, Mitch, waved from a distance.

"Look at you driving here to the park," she teased. She knew I lived just down the street.

"I know. It's my day to drop Tyson off at school."

She shook her head. I don't know if she disapproved or just didn't believe me.

"Ray, how are you today?" I met her eyes directly. This was more than just a superficial question.

She took a thoughtful breath. "You know, today is a good day. A very good day."

I hugged her, her earthy perfume soaking into my sleeves. "And why is that?"

"Well, I went in for one of my treatments last Friday. You see me sometimes walking no problem, and sometimes I have to sit. I wasn't here Saturday because it drained me. I could hardly walk the next day. But today I feel great."

"Your treatment? What kind of treatment? I didn't—"

"Blood cancer. It's my red blood cells. I have too many. It's a mutation that thickens my blood so bad my heart bogs down. I'll never die from the cancer; I'll die from the clots." She said it so matter-of-factly it was as if I had asked what type of dog biscuits she fed Mo.

"Oh, Ray," I said, ignoring the hand she held up.

"I don't want to hear—"

"You know, I have to tell you something. I see you every morning. You greet every person you meet with a smile and wish them a sincere good morning. Nobody does that anymore. We're all so buried in our phones and our problems we have a hard time looking up."

She smirked. "Well, my daddy always said the only reason not to talk to somebody in the morning is if you been in their face all night long."

I had heard that one before. It was one of her favorites. "I know, but it's 6:00 a.m. All of us here are half asleep, just starting the day. I see people light up when you talk to them. You make a difference. They look forward to your 'Good morning.' You are already a hero to them, but knowing that you—" I couldn't say it. I cleared my throat. "Do you know how special you are?" I choked on the last words, not realizing how much emotion they carried.

A wrinkled hand flew to her mouth. Tears trickled onto her cheeks, and she leaned forward, nudging the dogs out of the way. She kissed my cheek as she crushed me in a hug. "Oh, my baby girl. My baby girl." She turned to Mitch patiently waiting a few paces away. "Do you know my baby girl?"

"Ray, you call everyone baby girl," Mitch responded mechanically.

She put her hand on her right hip and wagged her head. "You didn't listen to what I said. This is MY baby girl. Mine."

Mitch raised a hand in surrender and picked up the dogs.

She turned back to me. "Do you want to know the last thing my mama told me before she died?"

"What was that?"

"She was lying there, out of it. The cancer had gone up to her brain by then. But she opened her eyes and looked at me, clear as day, and asked, 'Do you love me?' I looked into her eyes and said, 'Yes, Mama, I love you.' 'How much?' she asked. Well, when my boy, Alvin, was little, he used to go up to my mama, and she would ask him the same question. He'd count on his fingers and say, 'Grandma, I love you a million.' I turned to my mama then and said, 'Mama, I love you a million.' She told me, 'I love you a million more.' She went to sleep after that and died a couple of hours later. That was the last thing she said to me."

"Oh, wow, what an amazing memory."

"Baby girl, that stays with me. It's a part of me. I tell you what. You go home and you tell your boys that you love them so much it sticks to them. It stays with them. They will always know their mama loved them."

"I'll try." I could feel a lump in my throat and didn't trust myself to say anything more.

"You do it. Some days, they'll feel like they're not enough. In their lives, some may question their skin color. They won't be black enough, but they'll never be white. You grab them, hold them close, and let them know that no matter what, you love them. No matter what, God loves them. Make it stick."

"I will. I promise." I wiped my face on the sleeve of my running shirt.

She opened her fanny pack and pulled out a dog treat, then leaned down and handed it to Mo. She turned her head back to me. "You done?" she asked, eyebrows arched and waiting.

"Am I done? What do you mean?"

"Is your family done? You gonna try for more kids?"

I didn't need to think about it. I bit my lip to steady my voice. "No. No, we're not done. I know there's at least one more who still needs to be part of our family."

Ray nodded, her piercing eyes seeing more in me than I ever saw in myself. Maybe she knew. Maybe she understood. "Mmm-hmm." She whistled for Mo. "You make sure you introduce your new little one to us park relatives." She shuffled away, chiding Mitch for babying his "Kardashian" dog too much.

I smiled and walked in the opposite direction. I paused underneath the streetlight, stretching my legs in the dim yellow glow. I could have put in my earbuds and played something fast and loud. I could have timed my pace on my watch and tracked my heart rate. I didn't. The reverent power of Ray's story held my attention long after she'd called her dog to her side. I folded the earbuds into my pocket and walked the trail, music forgotten.

I knew my parents loved me the way Ray described. They were my fan club as I stood on the basketball court during the fourth quarter of the last game of the '95 season. I couldn't even move around yet, and they cheered for me. They rallied everyone in the stands. Both teams. They screamed so loud tears streamed down their cheeks. I didn't ever question that their love "stuck" to me. Every warm Banbury Cross doughnut solidified it.

I waved to Ronald as he retrieved the walker from the back of the car. He walked it around to Ellen and let her lean on his shoulder as she swung her legs to the side of the passenger seat and carefully put weight on her feet. I thought about how many times Keith let me lean on him, on his strength, on his faith, on his friendship. He'd seen the unhinged, black-mascara-streaked sobbing Chani who locked herself in the bathroom and ranted behind the door. And he still scribbled me pages of reasons why he admired me. And, oh, I loved him back! I loved him so much it scared me to think of a day without him. I placed his envelopes in the corners of my dresser mirror. I see those reminders every day. That kind of love sticks to me.

I walked around the baseball fields in silence, ready to hurdle the sprinklers if the timer went off unexpectedly. *It's no accident that I came to the park trail today instead of running through the neighborhood. I needed that conversation with Ray. I really did. God knew I needed it.* I stopped on the walkway, hands on my hips. I didn't need to catch my breath. For just a moment, I was alone. The rising sun warmed my cheeks. I took a deep, cleansing breath, letting my lungs absorb the oxygen. *So many coincidences. How can they be accidental?* I shook my head, hearing a dog collar jingle on the path behind me. *God loves me. There are so many reminders right in front of me. He's trying to make it stick.*

## Questions for the Reader:

*Is your faith contingent on getting what you want on your timeline?*

*Do you believe you are the primary architect of your life?*

*What can you do to better align your will with God's?*

# Conclusion

"So, what happened?" you might ask as you lean toward me, removing your sunglasses. "Did you ever find her?" You look earnestly into my eyes, trying to read my expression.

The corners of my mouth twitch as we pass the trailhead and wind our way toward the park to meet Keith and the boys. I nod toward a familiar stroller. I push aside the sunshade to reveal a mass of wild, dark hair protruding from underneath a pink-and-yellow blanket. I pull the blanket out and lay it over the arm of an empty bench. Tiny hands clasp underneath a delicate chin. You reach out and brush some of her hair off her porcelain cheek. She is beautiful. She is a miracle. But it's not what you think.

"Emmy girl! Ems!" Hudson barrels toward her, ramming into the stroller with his shoulder.

She startles, eyes wide, arms flying to brace against the sides of her comfortable nest. Her bottom lip threatens to curve into a pout until she sees Hudson's wide grin. Her sparkling eyes crinkle, and a coo gurgles from between her smiling lips. Huddy smuggles a pouch of fruit snacks from inside my bag and returns, triumphant, to where Keith stands near the slide.

I see the question in your eyes. No, she's not ours.

Some people wait in line for the newest gaming system on Black Friday. Others, a deal on a TV. We piled into the car in late November with scores of Thanksgiving ads littering the passenger seat. But an unexpected phone call shifted our holiday plans. We ended up at the hospital and brought home a baby girl. Our fourth foster child. The calm to our storm.

I reach over and maneuver a binky into her mouth. She gazes up at me, her smile poking out from behind her pacifier. I tuck her blanket around her and turn to catch the boys' attention. "Five minutes," I mouth to them.

You may be confused. I'm still figuring it out too.

The reality is, someday, she may go home. If that happens, I will pack her '50s cardigan and stuffed Snoopy doll into a duffel bag. I'll fold her clothes in tidy piles and wash all her special bottles. A notebook bulging with detailed health history and instructions will be handed off to a caseworker. I may never hear her hiccup-py cry again, and I might spend some days hiccup-py crying myself.

If that's the case, I'll treasure the healing she brought to my boys. I'm proud of the progress we've made through her endless medical visits and therapy appointments. We've made a difference. I've given my best. We've loved her without reservation. God has directed this process because we have had no say whatsoever.

But . . .

If she stays, my forever family will be complete. I will stand before a judge, lift my right hand, and swear that I will protect her as one of my own. She will adopt a new name. She will be ours. I will kneel at an altar in God's holy house and thank Him for His grace and guidance. Whatever the years bring, she will never question our love for her. It will stick.

I could have waited for a solid resolution before writing my story.

You might have finished this book expecting a fairy-tale realization of the amazing vision I experienced years before. Here's where I would have gladly inserted a picture of my little girl, my boys, and my husband.

But that's not the point.

I'm still in the middle of my journey. I don't have everything figured out. You're probably in the middle of your story. We're all writing our endings. I'd bet very few of us stand at the finish line, all loose ends neatly tied. But there's so much value in how far we've come!

Even though I don't know the final scene, I cling to what I do know.

I know a daughter will bless my life. I have no doubt of that. God promised me. I know He loves me. I trust Him completely, even if I don't always understand His timing. His story will finish exactly the way He planned it.

And so will yours . . .

# Thank You

Over the course of writing this book, an unexpected theme emerged as I tried to be open and vulnerable. Self-doubt and waning confidence blackened many of the pages. I knew I had experienced depression, but because I wasn't suicidal, I did not seek help, even when it was offered. But I'll be honest. Some days I scared myself. I didn't recognize myself.

So what helped?

I cannot speak for everyone, and I'm not a professional, but if you find yourself in a similar position, I've compiled a list of my own suggestions. You can find the free PDF download on my website at: www.ChaniBarlow.com. To express my gratitude to you for taking the time to read my story, I'm also including exclusive parenting insights, adoption stories, and faith-promoting tips in my newsletter.

I'd love to connect with you to hear about your experiences and the hard things you've overcome, big or small. Like I said, this book was written as a conversation between us. I can't wait to hear your side.

You can find me at:www.ChaniBarlow.com/contact

# About the Author

Chani Barlow is a typical messy ponytail, no makeup, T-shirt-and-jeans, writer/stay-at-home mommy. She survived a horrendous auto-pedestrian accident as a teenager that nearly took her life. She married her best friend, Keith Barlow, only to discover their "double curse" of infertility. They adopted three special boys and have fostered multiple additional children in Las Vegas, Nevada.

When Chani's not writing on the floor of her bedroom with her dog cuddled up against her legs, you might find her pacing behind the bleachers during her son's baseball game. Or, she's lip syncing to Kelly Clarkson as she rounds the jogging trail at the park. Then again, she could be lounging in a lawn chair as her kids soak the driveway with a garden hose. In any situation, if you offer her one of your peanut M&Ms, you'll find a friend for life!

# End Notes

This book is a true story, as honestly as I can remember the details. I have changed most of the names of the people and agencies involved to protect their privacy. The dialogue in this book is not verbatim (especially in conversations that occurred decades ago), but I tried to capture the overall tone, general ideas, and results. The conversations that occur toward the end of the book are incredibly accurate, as I went home and wrote them directly after they took place.

I acknowledge that this story is a result of my perception of the events in my life. I apologize if I have misunderstood or misrepresented anyone in any way.

Thank you for taking the time to read it.

1   "How Firm a Foundation," Hymns (Salt Lake City, Utah: The Church of Jesus Christ of Latter-day Saints, 1985), 85, used with permission, Intellectual Reserve, Inc."

2   "Where Can I Turn for Peace?" Hymns (Salt Lake City, Utah: The Church of Jesus Christ of Latter-day Saints, 1985), 129, used with permission, Intellectual Reserve, Inc."

3   Matt 20:4 KJV

# A free ebook edition is available with the purchase of this book.

**To claim your free ebook edition:**

1. Visit MorganJamesBOGO.com
2. Sign your name CLEARLY in the space
3. Complete the form and submit a photo of the entire copyright page
4. You or your friend can download the ebook to your preferred device

A **FREE** ebook edition is available for you or a friend with the purchase of this print book.

_____

CLEARLY SIGN YOUR NAME ABOVE

**Instructions to claim your free ebook edition:**
1. Visit MorganJamesBOGO.com
2. Sign your name CLEARLY in the space above
3. Complete the form and submit a photo of this entire page
4. You or your friend can download the ebook to your preferred device

## Print & Digital Together Forever.

Snap a photo

Free ebook

Read anywhere

CPSIA information can be obtained
at www.ICGtesting.com
Printed in the USA
JSHW021442100622
26950JS00001B/4

9 781631 957963